THE ISLANDS OF BOSTON HARBOR

EDWARD ROWE SNOW

THE ISLANDS
OF
BOSTON HARBOR
1630-1971

ILLUSTRATED

DODD, MEAD & COMPANY
NEW YORK

Third Printing

ISBN: 0-396-06436-1
Library of Congress Catalog Card Number: 71-169730

Printed in the United States of America
by The Cornwall Press, Inc., Cornwall, N.Y.

To the three women of my life
My wife, Anna-Myrle
Our daughter, Dorothy
And our granddaughter, Laura

INTRODUCTION

The first edition of my first book, *Islands of Boston Harbor*, was published in 1935, and before the year ended it had sold so well it was out of print. Then came the second edition the following year. That edition was completely exhausted in an amazingly short time. As the years went by five different volumes on the same general subject were written, and each in turn was sold out. They were *Sailing Down Boston Bay*, *The Romance of Boston Bay*, *Secrets of the North Atlantic Islands*, *Legends, Maps, and Stories*, and *New England Sea Drama*, which was reprinted nine times. Each of the above volumes is now a collector's item.

Therefore, in this year of 1971, or thirty-six years after my first book on the subject, I am bringing the history and romance of Boston Harbor, along with the legends and supernatural tales, up to date.

I am grateful to all of you who read these words for making this new book on Boston Harbor possible. In addition to those who have requested anonymity, I mention the following who have helped me in this my seventy-first book: William Alcott, Thelma S. Allen, Charles Berger, Dorothy Caroline Snow Bicknell, T. Frank Brennan, Mary Brown, James L. Bruce, Curtis Chase, Josephine Cobb, Madeleine Connors, George F. Coombs, Arthur J. Cunningham, Richard Dean, Captain Charles Denny, Girard Edwards, Walter Spahr Ehrenfeld, Alfred Ela, Charles Eskrigge, Chester A. Fazakas, Leo Flaherty, Laura Gibbs, Captain Joseph Gilbreth, Eleanor Gregory, Marie Hansen, Barbara Hayward, Ethel Hazleton, John R. Herbert, Melina Herron, Charles O. Hurd, Captain J. I. Kemp, Joseph Kolb, Gary Kosciusko, Lorraine Langley, Captain George P. Lord, Sergeant Enoch W. Lyman, William Francis McIntire, Warren Manning, George R. Marvin, Maggie Mills, Major J. W. H. Myrick, Joel O'Brien, F. Ward Paine, Franklin Pierce, William Pyne, Helen Salkowski, Grace Saphir, Hugh J. Shaw, Fitz-Henry Smith, Jr., Alice Rowe Snow, Donald B. Snow, Florence Snow, Winthrop Snow, Edith Stevens, Albert V. Stolpe, Benjamin Stewart, George P. Tilton, Colonel Roland Tilton, John G. Weld, Eber M. Wells, Daisy Whitman, Captain William Wincapaw, and Charles R. O. Wood.

Fred Clow should be mentioned for his faithful photographic efforts through the years.

My wife, Anna-Myrle, as usual, responded with her unselfish spirit.

Institutions made my task easier, among them the following: Ventress Memorial Library, Marshfield; the Allen and the Peirce Memorial Libraries of Scituate; the Boston Athenaeum; the Boston Public Library; the Thomas Crane Public Library of Quincy; the Harvard College Library; the Bostonian Society; the Society for the Preservation of New England Antiquities; the Massachusetts Archives; the Peabody Museum; the American Antiquarian Society in

Worcester; the Essex Institute; the Massachusetts Marine Historical League; the National Archives; the Boston Marine Society; the Massachusetts Historical Society; the Maine Historical Society; the Nathan Tufts Library in Weymouth; and *Yankee* magazine. The late Robb Sagendorph, as always, was an inspiration.

Due acknowledgment should be given to Nathaniel Bradstreet Shurtleff and Moses Foster Sweetser for their outstanding books written generations ago on Boston Harbor.

I sincerely trust that before the reader has visited the last "happy isle," he will share some of the deep love I have for the islands and lighthouses of Boston Harbor.

EDWARD ROWE SNOW

CONTENTS

ILLUSTRATIONS

1

GEORGE'S ISLAND—
FORT WARREN

America, the new world, compares in glamour and romance with the old, and Boston Harbor is one of the most delightful places in America.

For many years historians have wondered whether Thorwald the Norseman visited the New England coast as far south as Massachusetts Bay. If this bold Viking leader of nine centuries ago did reach the site of what is now Boston, he was the first European to look out over Boston Harbor.

Captain John Smith left us an interesting map of Massachusetts Bay which was probably used by Myles Standish on his exploring trip to Boston Harbor in 1621. When the Puritans founded Boston, John Winthrop made a map of the islands and surrounding shoreline; his chart represents a substantial improvement over the map of Captain Smith. The next real attempt to survey the islands occurred about fifty-five years later when Thomas Pound drew his very satisfactory chart. This map was universally copied for many years.

Each island in Boston Harbor has had its own period of

importance in the history of Boston and Massachusetts. Deer Island and Long Island are still vital parts of Boston's city government, and Governor's Island was the famous John Winthrop's home in Puritan days. Nix's Mate and Bird Island were prominent during the pirate era, while Fort Independence on Castle Island saw its only battle during the Revolution. George's Island will always be associated with the days of the Civil War, or the War between the States as the Southerners like to call it. Fort Warren, located on this island since 1833, has more memories of the Civil War days than any other place in New England. Seven miles to the eastward of Boston, between Lovell's and Rainsford's Islands, it is the strategic center of Boston Harbor.

The activity George's Island saw between 1861 and 1865 was varied and spectacular with soldiers, prisoners, and even ghosts figuring in the events of the period. Hundreds of soldiers who trained at Fort Warren left the island never *1,000 +* to return; over one thousand Confederates were imprisoned in the walls of this historic old fortress. Many attempts at escape were made here, none of which, as far as is known, was completely successful. This fort was the prison of Mason and Slidell in 1861, and four years later held Alexander Stephens in captivity. *✓ Pres Confederacy*

Going back to the days before the Puritans arrived in Boston Harbor, we find that James Pemberton owned George's Island. It was then known as Pemberton's Island, and when its ownership was in question in 1652, Pemberton produced proof that he had come to the island two years before the Puritans arrived and had been living there ever since. The Court accepted his proof and declared Pemberton's Island "to be his propriety." We do not know when Pemberton left the island which bore his name for almost a century, but the date of his death was February 5, 1682.

In 1690 Samuel Sewall and a group of officers went down the Harbor to George's Island. This party of dignitaries from Boston watched the English flotilla maneuver in the Road and observed the muster held on the island itself. The fleet later sailed away under Sir William Phips to participate in the disastrous expedition against Canada.

In 1709 new preparations were made to receive another flotilla. On May 2 of that year the council voted to "cause one or more sheds to contain in all 100 feet in length, 15 feet wide and seven feet high to be raised on George's Island to receive and Lodge the sick amongst her Majesty's Forces speedily expected to arrive here from England."

The fleet did not come, however, since it was diverted to Portuguese waters, and during the next summer one of the barracks was "burnt down by some ill-minded person or persons." Adam Winthrop, the captain at the Castle went to George's Island and brought the remaining barracks back to Castle Island. The fleet did arrive at Boston Harbor in 1711, with Sir Hovendon Walker at the head of a mighty squadron which anchored in the Harbor. After hasty arrangements had been completed, George's Island was used as the hospital base for the sick soldiers of Marlborough's regiments which had accompanied the fleet. The rest of the troops were encamped on Noddle's Island.

The next time George's Island received notice was during the Revolution. When the British evacuated Boston, they did not leave the Harbor for some time, but sailed around the islands week after week. Dr. William McKinstry, a prominent Taunton Tory who had been obliged to flee Boston just before the fighting started, had been active in dressing the wounds of the injured British soldiers after the Lexington engagement and was now placed aboard one of the British ships. Ill when the fleet sailed, he grew worse as the weeks passed, dying on board ship in Nantasket Road. His body was taken to George's Island and buried there.

The British left Boston so unexpectedly that they could not notify England in time to stop many of the transport ships which had already started for Boston. On the first anniversary of the battle of Bunker Hill two transports just off the shore of Pemberton's former residence were attacked by the Americans. The transports that had sailed unsuspectingly into Boston Harbor were the ship *George*, with six cannon and 114 Highlanders under Colonel Campbell, and the brigantine *Annabella* carrying seventy-four Highlanders besides her regular crew. At midnight the American vessels approached the two English troopships and hailed the *George*, demanding that she surrender. They were refused, and a fierce struggle began which lasted till dawn. When Colonel Campbell saw that defeat was near, he tore his regimental colors into bits and threw them overboard. The British Major Menzies and eight Highlanders were killed on the *George*, while one soldier met his death on the *Annabella*. The American ship that took a very active part in the battle was the *Warren*, which nicely matched the English vessel *George* since the battle was fought off the shores of George's Island where Fort Warren is now located.

The British continued their supremacy over France on the high seas, however, and Lord Howe gave that nation another crushing defeat off Newport in 1778. The French commander brought his battered ships into Boston Harbor. Chevalier, in his fine history of the French Navy, tells us that the "garrisons of vessels and detachments of sailors, debarked on George and Nantasket Islands, worked immediately on the construction of batteries destined to defend the anchorage. . . . September 1, we had on George Island six mortars and two batteries, the one of eleven pieces of cannon of twenty-four, and the other of eighteen at twenty-four." The largest of the frigates, the *Cesar*, had been terribly damaged in the encounter with the British ships.

At the turn of the century, Thomas Crane was born at his father's farm on the island, and later in life he became a leading New York capitalist.

Frederick W. A. S. Brown wrote the following stanzas about George's Island shortly after his visit in the spring of 1819:

> *Of George's Isle; oh muse, now speak,*
> *Whose lofty southern shore*
> *Secures a ship from whirlwinds bleak,*
> *Until the storm is o'er.*
>
> *Here, too, the passenger may find,*
> *Whate'er his taste can please;*
> *A book to entertain his mind,*
> *And unaffected ease.*

Frederick Brown was quite interested in a young lady whom he met on what he called "George's happy shore," but we shall never know the details of this island courtship. For some reason he did not win the girl of his dream, but after returning from his final visit to George's Island penned the thoughts of his lady fair. He hoped that he would

> *Oft recall each fleeting scene*
> *Of pleasure and delight*
> *Her fancy formed, while o'er the green*
> *She strayed at morn or night.*

He does not tell us her name, so perhaps she was the original "Lady in Black" of George's Island.

The Government began work in 1826 on the seawall at

George's Island. Doctor Jerome Van Crowninshield Smith, then Port Physician at Rainsford's Island, visited the men who were constructing the wall. Smith tells us that $52,000 had already been appropriated by the Government at this time. The sea wall was built on the east and northeast side of the island. He goes on to say that "We may expect to see a fort in the outer harbor that will bid defiance to all the ships of war that ever sailed."

The Government began the survey of the island and started work on the fort in 1833, when the name Warren was taken from the fortifications at Governor's Island and applied to the works at George's Island.

Writer Peter Peregrine sailed by Fort Warren on July 30, 1838. The workmen had already been laboring five years, and the results shown on the island so impressed him that he said it suggested a sort of "Ocean Thermopylae, where a small band of Boston Yankees would as triumphantly beat back the navy of Great Britain as did the 'Immortal Three Hundred' the myriads of Xerxes." In making a comparison between Fort Warren and the Rock of Gibraltar, he thought that the fortress on George's Island commanded the entrance to Boston Harbor far more effectively than the famous rock controlled the entrance to the Mediterranean Sea.

James Lloyd Homer, one of the early contributors to the *Boston Post,* wrote under the pseudonym of the "Shade of Alden." He first visited the island with a "matrimonial party" from Weymouth in August 1845. We quote from the survey he made of the fort at that time.

"As far as the Fort is finished, it is probably the most magnificent piece of masonry in this or in any other country. . . . The dry-dock at Charlestown is a splendid piece of workmanship, but it bears no comparison to the Fort at

George's Island, the foundation walls of which are twelve feet thick, and the superstructure eight. . . ."

The principal material used was Quincy granite, with granite from Cape Ann for filling purposes. One gun comprised the entire defense at this time, and in June 1848, that one cannon still stood alone as a challenge to an invading navy. Incidentally, conditions were not much better in 1857, for according to an illustration in *Ballou's Pictorial*, the platforms on the shore were not equipped with guns of any sort. Even at the start of the Civil War, Fort Warren was practically worthless for defensive purposes.

James Lloyd Homer made a careful survey of the whole fortress on his visit in 1845. A Mr. Gould brought shipload after shipload of supplies for the hungry workmen. He kept a large herd of cows and many hogs which rambled over the slopes of Pemberton's old island.

Homer's story of his visit to the semi-subterranean prison is the most interesting part of the account of his trip to Fort Warren. Let us accompany him on his journey. Starting at the parapets:

"You descend a long flight of stone steps. Having touched the ground, you walk about forty feet, and then turn to the left, when you find yourself in the 'prisonhouse' of the Fort, which extends, through several apartments or sections, a distance of over one hundred feet, and is capable of accommodating one thousand prisoners, if we should ever have as many in New England, which is at least problematical—unless the foul fiends disunion and insurrection should raise their bloody and unsightly crests on the soil of the Pilgrims."

The rooms through which he traveled that day really held hundreds of Confederate soldiers during the Civil War. The stairway which the "Shade of Alden" used to enter the prison dungeons has been walled up and the only entrance today is through a small carronade embrasure reached by ladder from outside the walls of the fort.

An interested visitor to Fort Warren landed from the 42-ton sloop *General Warren* on October 13, 1853, after a run of one hour. Thomas Kelah Wharton, who was later to assist Beauregard in the construction of the great New Orleans Custom House, was met at the pier by Sylvanus Thayer himself. A few lines from Wharton follow:

"We sailed forth to explore the fortifications—and first took the circuit of the outer parapet, rising to the height of 69 feet above tide water, enclosing an area of about 12 acres, and faced with Granite, beautifully cut, and jointed, and 8 feet in thickness. On this exposed elevation the wind tried hard to rob us of our hats and cloaks, but it was so pure and healthy I should have been sorry had there been less of it. We descended one of the exquisitely cut spiral staircases to the 'Quarters.' "

With the start of the war in April 1861, Governor John Albion Andrew visited George's Island. The salute due him had to be postponed until the soldiers could find enough ammunition to fire it off. The *Alabama* could easily have run the gauntlet of Fort Warren and Castle Island to drop a few shells on Beacon Hill.

Fort Warren was the birthplace of the greatest Yankee song, *John Brown's Body*. It was the product of the 2nd Infantry, or Tiger Battalion. The Battalion, composed of four companies under the command of Major Ralph Newton, arrived at Fort Warren on April 29, 1861.

The members of the "Tigers" found great heaps of earth lying around inside the parade ground, and it was made clear to the men that their first job would be to put the fortress into proper shape for military occupancy. Since the soldiers were of high social standing and manual labor was entirely foreign to them, only the knowledge that they were helping their country kept them at work.

Singing seemed to be the best way for the men to pass their time while working. A really fine chorus was the result. Religious hymns were just as popular as secular songs, and the favorite hymn sung at the fort grew to be *Say, Brothers, Will You Meet Us?* From this hymn, sung time and time again, came the tune chosen by the composers of *John Brown's Body.*

The story of the manner in which the words were written and put to music is interesting. The man who led the raid on Harper's Ferry in 1859 had a Scotch namesake in the Tiger Battalion. John Brown always joined in the fun at Fort Warren, and when it was realized that he had the same name as the abolitionist hanged near Harper's Ferry, the others lost no time in making him the object of their remarks. Whenever he chanced to be a few minutes later than the rest at one of their gatherings, they told him to arrive on time if he wished to free the slaves. At another time he was told that he couldn't be John Brown, for John Brown's body was mouldering in the grave. John Brown, the Scotchman, helped compose the song with Newton Pernette, J. E. Greenleaf, C. S. Hall, and C. B. Marsh, all of whom were active in its preparation.

While the song *John Brown's Body* was still in its infancy, the 12th Massachusetts Regiment, commanded by Fletcher Webster, came to Fort Warren. In a short time the tune was known by the whole regiment, having spread from company to company. The Brigade Band had been coming down to the island to play for the soldiers many Sundays, and in some manner the band leader had obtained a copy of the melody. One Sunday night the regiment and the battalion were scheduled for a joint dress parade, and as the band swung into line the musicians electrified the gathering by striking up *John Brown's Body*.

This was the first time the song was ever played by a military band. Shortly afterward the government notified the Tiger Battalion that only organizations of ten companies or over could be accepted for active service at the front, and so the soldiers disbanded. Many of the men, however, now joined the 12th, and John Brown and Newton Pernette were among them. When the 11th and 14th Regiments came to the Fort, they also enjoyed singing the song even after the Tigers had left the island.

On July 18, 1861, the Webster Regiment, as it was called, visited Boston for a grand review and was met at the dock by the 2nd Battalion. While marching up State Street, the band struck up the tune of *John Brown's Body*, and every man in the line joined in. The effect was startling, and the crowds watching the parade were greatly impressed by the swing of the tune. The regiment caused a sensation in New York, arousing the populace with the stirring rhythm of the new song.

When the 14th Regiment left Fort Warren and went to Washington, Abraham Lincoln and Julia Ward Howe visited the camp of the Massachusetts soldiers. The stirring strains of *John Brown's Body* so moved Lincoln that Julia Ward Howe was asked to compose a hymn from the tune. *The Battle Hymn of the Republic* was her inspired answer.

The crowds went wild everywhere when they heard the magical strains of *John Brown's Body*, and the melody soon reached the far corners of the Union. On June 6, 1862, John Brown, the Scotchman, then serving with the Massachusetts Volunteers, went to his death in the Shenandoah River, Virginia. Thus passed the man who was indirectly responsible for the greatest marching song of the Civil War.

When the Massachusetts men were going through Baltimore on their way to battle, several were killed by shots from the crowd. Scores of politicians were arrested, taken to Fort Lafayette, and later moved on the *State of Maine* to Fort Warren. Among the political prisoners taken to George's Island was Lawrence Sangston, a former member of the Maryland Legislature. He had been confined with over one hundred other Southern civilians at Fort Lafayette. Accompanied by several hundred Confederate soldiers, the political prisoners had sailed for Fort Warren arriving late at night on October 31, 1861. In his diary Sangston shows much of the war-time bitterness evidenced by both sides during the conflict.

The next morning Sangston arose early and began to realize that the prisoners were going to be accorded better treatment than they had received at Fort Lafayette. "The officers appear to understand their position," he tells us, and goes on to express his delight with the speed in which the supplies ordered from Boston were received. Later in the day a driving northeast snowstorm set in during which the men were forced to stay inside the casemates. At the same time, miles out in Massachusetts Bay, the luckless square-rigger *Maritana* was plunging through ever-increasing seas that were to send her to her doom on Shag Rocks before the next sunrise. Sangston's last entry for the day is significant:

"Storm increasing, fearful night for ships on the coast; at times the wind would whistle through the casemate windows equal to the shrill whistle of a locomotive engine, and after listening an hour to the howling of the storm, and the waves breaking over the rocks, went to sleep."

The next day was Sunday, and at ten o'clock the gale ceased. Several of the North Carolina prisoners who were allowed to walk along the ramparts returned to Sangston's quarters with the fearful news of a marine tragedy near Boston Light. It was the *Maritana*, which had piled up on Shag Rocks in the blinding storm early that morning. The North Carolina soldiers reported that they had seen the nude body of a woman being recovered from the spit of sand that runs from Greater Brewster Island.

Sangston tells us that on the fifth of November he enjoyed a "regular Yankee breakfast; codfish and potatoes, baked beans and pumpkin 'sass,' all very good except the coffee." Again commenting on the good treatment received at Fort Warren, he wrote that he experienced "none of the rudeness and insolence we had to encounter daily at Fort Lafayette."

The following week, Colonel Pegram, aided by Captain De Lagnel and Charles H. Pitts, took his turn at running the mess operated by the wealthier prisoners. This was the week Sangston received a large package from home containing liquor of various assortments. Colonel Dimmick permitted him to keep the liquor, advising him to use the same in a judicious manner. His friends were all suddenly seized with anxiety about Sangston's health which could only "be relieved by personal inquiry."

In spite of the many storms at the island and regardless of the strain under which the prisoners lived, there were many enjoyable days at the fort. Sangston's diary gives us a fine account of life in the casemates:

"At half-past four, when we leave the parade ground and retire to our rooms, and the sentinels are drawn into our door, I trim and light my lamp, and prepare my writing table for those who wish to write, or read in quiet, leaving the front room for conversation, and the backgammon players, the only game we have, as there are not enough card players among us to make up a game; at ten o'clock, I brew a pitcher of hot whiskey punch, which we sip until eleven; Colonel Pegram, the only one among us who does not partake of the punch, gives us some very fine music from his guitar, and we put out the light and go to bed."

The first rumors regarding Mason and Slidell reached Fort Warren the twenty-third of November. The two Confederate Commissioners, captured at sea on November 8, 1861, arrived on November 24 and were quartered in the front room of Quarters Number Seven, adjacent to the small room Sangston was then occupying. Their secretaries, McFarland and Eustis, were also quartered with the commissioners. McFarland had an excellent voice, and would sing to the accompaniment of his guitar. The last entry for November 27, 1861, reads:

"Colonel Pegram and Mr. McFarland entertained us with some fine singing and music on the guitar, which they continued long after the lights were put out, and we went to bed."

Colonel Pegram became the famous General John Pegram after his exchange, and was killed in a battle near Petersburg.

A great gale lashed the island on December 28, preventing the Boston boat from landing, and the day seemed long without fresh reading matter. Sangston, however, was soon to have a surprise. The very next day Colonel Dimmick informed him that he was to be given a thirty-day leave from Fort Warren. Mason and Slidell also received word of their coming release the same day.

International law was a favorite topic during the stay of the Commissioners, and Mason predicted almost exactly the date when the United States would release them. Late in December, President Lincoln gave special orders for their freedom, to take effect January 1, 1862. Because of the disturbance a few weeks before when some other prisoners had been released, Colonel Dimmick took steps to insure a silent departure when the commissioners should leave the Fort.

January 1, 1862 proved to be a stormy day with great seas sweeping around the island. The wharf was under water at high tide, and, when the Confederate party left the dock on a small tugboat, there was some doubt as to whether they would reach Provincetown in safety. But the tug *Starlight* transferred its cargo in Provincetown Harbor to the British 16-gun man-of-war *Rinaldo* and returned to Boston. Thus Fort Warren saw the last of "lean, dyspeptic" Slidell and "portly, jovial" Mason.

An incident in the celebration at Fort Warren of the surrender of Fort Donelson should interest the reader. Colonel Dimmick, whom soldiers and prisoners alike admired, left the island, believing the men could celebrate to better advantage in his absence. Salutes were prepared and all was in readiness when the bandmaster of the 1st Artillery presented himself at headquarters to ask a favor. He had fired the last gun in the surrender of Fort Sumter, he said, and he wished to be the first to fire a salute in honor of the Donelson victory. His wish was granted, and as he went to his station the bandmaster was given a great cheer by the men assembled on the parade ground. A week later prisoners from Fort Donelson, including General Simon B. Buckner and General Lloyd Tilghman, arrived at Fort Warren.

On the twenty-seventh of May, 1862, the Independent Corps of Cadets, sometimes called the Boston Cadets and often designated as the First Corps Cadets, was called out for active service by Governor Andrew. Hastily assembling at their old armory opposite the Granary Burying Grounds, the cadets formed in line and marched to Long Wharf where they boarded the boat for Fort Warren.

After a sail down the Harbor they landed at George's Island, meeting Colonel Dimmick at the dock. Dimmick was greatly surprised at the fine red and gray uniforms the men wore and wondered what type of military organization it was that could have a colonel, an adjutant, and two majors in a total membership of slightly over one hundred. The Boston Cadets soon discarded their showy but then unpopular gray uniforms for the blue of the army.

The rats at the fort must be mentioned. They were in complete charge of the casemates at night, and their tails, according to the men, were as large as a man's little finger. Perhaps they were the descendants of the rats that had lived at George's Island since 1709 and had been multiplying ever since the old barracks were erected. They were a great nuisance. A certain member of the Corps had occasion to remember them for many years to come. This soldier, who had been given permission to spend the day in the city, returned to the fort on the afternoon boat, his hair slicked down with barber's oil. Weary from his holiday in the city, he retired early and dreamed that night of countless mosquitoes stinging his head, but he did not awaken. The next morning when the drumbeat aroused the fort, the young cadet jumped out of bed to find his hair neatly removed. The rats, greedy for the barber's oil, had mowed his head as smoothly as could be desired, and the poor soldier was bald for the rest of his days.

The gayest affair at the island was the Cadet Ball, the like of which, it is safe to say, has never been seen since. As the ladies could not be present in person, some of the young men took their places. We are told that the Misses Wellman, Inches, and Goodwin, all socially prominent, were very attractive in their costumes, but Mrs. Barlow was "the belle of the ball."

There were many notable prisoners confined at Fort Warren during the war. George Proctor Kane, the Baltimore chief of police, had been sent north after the famous riots in that city. After his release, Kane became mayor of Baltimore and died in 1878 while in office.

General Simon Bolivar Buckner, an old West Point professor, was brought here in February 1862, after his surrender of Fort Donelson. Just before the surrender, Buckner received the famous message from General Grant: "No terms except an unconditional and immediate surrender can be accepted."

The capture of two Confederate warships in June 1863 was the first step in a dramatic incident which aroused all New England two months later. The Confederate battleship *Tacony* was taken on the twenty-seventh of June, while the *Atlanta* had been captured by the *U.S.S. Weehauken* ten days earlier. The officers and crew of the two captured ships were taken to Fort Warren where they were practically forgotten until a daring escape on the night of August 19, 1863, excited New England.

Lieutenant Joseph W. Alexander of the *Atlanta* was the first to discover the exit which was later used in the thrilling escape from Fort Warren. Naturally he was anxious to get back to the scene of activity and was constantly on the alert for a chance to leave the island. One day he was standing in the pump room under the quarters where the men lived, looking through the loophole at the grass on the cover face. The thought occurred to him that it might be possible to squeeze through the seven-inch musketry loophole. He climbed up into the opening and was pleased to find that he could push his head through the slit. As his clothing prevented him from getting his body out, he removed his outer garments and tried again. This time he was gratified to find that he could squeeze through the aperture. Being small in stature, as is shown by his picture, he realized that only men of slight build would be able to escape by this method.

After telling the others of the discovery, he found there were only three men in the quarters who were able to go through the opening. They were Captain Charles W. Reed, who had been commander of the *Tacony* at the time of its capture, Lieutenant James Thurston of the *Atlanta*, and Major Reid Saunders, a quartermaster in the Confederate army.

On Sunday night, August 16, 1863, they made an attempt at escape. A wild northeaster was blowing, and the night was very dark. After tying together a rope from their canvas bags, they lowered themselves out of the loopholes and were soon on the floor of the dry moat. The quartet cautiously made their way up the inner surface of the cover face and quietly slipped down the outer slope. At the foot of their descent was a small thicket, where they hid to plan the escape from the island itself.

After carefully surveying the situation, they made their way across the open space in the direction of a wooden target which stood on the beach a few rods from the thicket. They planned to push it off into the water, and swim their way across the Narrows until they reached Lovell's Island. Alexander knew of a fine sailboat belonging to Mr. Barber pulled up on the beach at Lovell's Island, a half mile away. Placing the target into the water, the four men jumped in and bravely started kicking their way across what was then the main ship channel.

Soon they became so benumbed and confused by the combination of water, wind, and huge waves, that they gave up the unequal struggle and let the ocean push them back on the beach. Putting the target back into place, they were successful in returning to their quarters without discovery.

The next day the four men formulated plans for a release which they hoped would be successful. If two strong swimmers could be found in some of the other quarters, they reasoned, the pair could swim across to Lovell's Island, get the sailboat, and sail it back to the fort, where the four officers would board it. Two prisoners were found who claimed to be good swimmers: N. B. Pryde of the *Tacony*, and Thomas Sherman, formerly a sailor in the United States navy. They were given full instructions, and everything was in readiness for the next try for freedom. When the night of August 19 began dark and threatening, every prisoner knew the break would be attempted. At about nine-fifteen the four men started to climb out of the casemates. All was quiet until Alexander inadvertently knocked over a bottle, which crashed onto the granite floor with a noise that he feared must have been heard by the guard at the main sally port. There was a challenge from the sentry; the prisoners shivered. Alexander looked over at the bridge and found it was merely an officer passing into the sally port. Because of the rising west wind, the crash of the bottle had not been heard. With great relief the four men now climbed down into the moat and made for the meeting-place at the top of the demilune. Pryde and Sherman were waiting for them, having successfully escaped from their part of the bastion.

It was then agreed that Reed and Saunders should wait in the shelter of the demilune while the four others would make their way down to the shore. Evading the sentries, the four men reached the beach. The two swimmers stripped off their clothing, and after a word of farewell, plunged into the dark waters. That farewell, as far as can be discov-

ered, were the last words ever spoken by the two men, as
no trace of them has been found to this day. F. A. Boles,
writing of the escape in 1864, said that nothing had been
heard from them. No facts have as yet been presented to
substantiate the belief that the men were successful in
reaching the South. The strong west wind probably proved
too much for the swimmers, sweeping them out to sea.

When the two men failed to return, Reed and Saunders
joined Thurston and Alexander. The latter, desperate in
their disappointment, agreed to take the target out again
while Reed and Saunders were to stay behind to wait for
the other two to return in the sailboat. Placing the target in
the water, the two men were soon kicking their way in the
general direction of Lovell's Island. Perhaps the wind had
changed, possibly the tide had turned—no matter—they were
successful in reaching their goal. Walking along the beach
at Lovell's Island, they finally located Mr. Barber's boat
and struggled to get it into the water. After spending half
an hour in a vain effort to move the sailboat, Alexander
discovered that it was tied to the anchor at the stern and
soon released the anchor. Sliding the craft over the stones
into the water, they jumped into the boat and hoisted sail.
By this time the first streaks of dawn were showing over
Boston Light, and the men realized it was too late to go
back for Reed and Saunders.

Reed and Saunders had crouched in the shadow of the
seawall near the hole where the target had been. A sentinel
came along and fell into the hole. His shouts caused the
other sentry to walk over to find out what was wrong. The
two men debated about where the target had gone, finally
concluding that it had been blown away. They peered over
the edge of the seawall and saw a dark mass, actually the two
prisoners, below them. Believing that it might be the target,

one of the men pricked at the mass with his bayonet, but as it yielded under his prods, he concluded it was seaweed and not the lost target. He ceased his effort, saying that he didn't wish to have rust from the salty seaweed on his bayonet. To the relief of the men crouching under the seawall, the sentries now returned to their posts. But dawn was rapidly approaching, and they realized that they must go back to their prison. They ran across the open ground on their way to the moat, but the guard caught sight of them and aroused the entire post. Reed and Saunders were captured and soon placed in solitary confinement.

Thurston and Alexander in the meantime had laid a course straight up the coast and when morning came were in the vicinity of Cape Ann. They went ashore but were not able to obtain help. The next morning they landed at Rye Beach and were successful in purchasing overalls and hats. Setting their course for St. John, they were far out off Portland when chased and captured by a U.S. revenue cutter, the *Dobbin*. After a brief stay in the jail, where the people came to see the "rebels from Fort Warren" as if they were animals in a zoo, they were returned to George's Island on September 7, 1863, not quite three weeks from the time of their escape. Colonel Dimmick now had iron bars set into the stonework of each musketry loophole in the casemates occupied by the naval prisoners. This precaution did not prevent two other escapes from the island before the war ended, and we shall now discuss the first of these two tries for freedom.

The first escape occurred in October 1863, and was from the demilune outside the fort. Ever since 1875 the soldier-guides have pointed out the block of granite set into the casemate openings of the *caponnière*, or demilune, located outside the main sally port. The original granite work had been chipped away, and a block was set into the opening. The guides have told the story of the Confederate soldier shot while trying to escape there, and I have heard that Mason and Slidell were shot while trying to climb out of this particular musketry loophole! There is, of course, no historical evidence to substantiate either of these two stories, but I have found definite proof of the manner in which the granite window sill was chipped away.

A deserter from a Maine regiment had been sentenced to two years' confinement at Fort Warren. This man, Private Sawyer, worked for three weeks chiseling away the edges of the granite loophole. Setting fire to newspapers he put in the slot, Sawyer waited until the granite was red hot. He then threw water on the stone and little by little the granite flaked off. As soon as the opening was large enough for his body, his comrades lowered him by a small rope out of the loophole twenty feet above the mud in the ditch. The rope, frayed by the sharp edge of the granite, suddenly broke, dropping him in the remaining distance to the moat. He saw the lights of a schooner lying at anchor in George's Island Road. After a swim out to the vessel, he secreted himself on board. The ship sailed away at about two in the morning, and Sawyer gave himself up shortly before 10 A.M. The schooner was the *C. W. Dyer* under Captain Pierce, and as soon as the captain learned all the particulars of Sawyer's escape, he sailed into New Bedford Harbor and turned Sawyer over to the police. Sawyer was executed as a deserter.

The same year an irate pilot of Boston Harbor complained to the Government of the treatment he had received from the guards at Fort Warren. Henry Hunt, during a heavy fog, had passed the island in a canoe on the way to pilot a ship anchored near the fort. The guards at the fort fired a volley at him, but he escaped uninjured. He shouted his objections, and was treated to another volley which pierced the canoe. His pride conquered, he now gave up the unequal fight and paddled away into the fog out of sight of the alert sentries at the island.

We now come to the unusual story of the cabin boy of the unfortunate *Atlanta*'s crew, McBlair by name. This fifteen-year-old lad used to sit in the casemates, dreaming of almost forgotten days in the south, when one day a kind soldier brought him a book to read. It was Alexander Dumas' famous *Count of Monte Cristo*. The young cabin boy suddenly developed the spirit of a lion and determined to escape from the island. One day he hid away behind a Parrott gun on the parapet, but the guards discovered him in time. On another occasion he dressed himself in some old rags which the laborers had discarded and had actually stepped on the gangplank of a boat to Boston when detected by one of the guards.

His third attempt at leaving the island was made about eleven months after the six men had escaped through the musketry loopholes. Late one night he crawled through the narrow window and let himself down by a small rope which parted and dropped him into the moat. Severely injured, he crawled into the water and started to swim away from the island. The water was so cold and his injuries pained him so greatly that he finally had to call for help. A boat was launched, and the injured boy was brought back to the prison in an unconscious condition.

On the twenty-second of July, 1864, Historian Edward A. Pollard, a captured Southerner, was permitted to walk along the shore outside of the fort itself, and came upon the grave of Edward J. Johnston, who had died in October of the previous year. Johnston, before his death, had requested that his head be faced toward the South, and his dying wish was granted. Years later the body was removed to Governor's Island, where this request was again honored, but in 1908 when the body was moved to Deer Island, the wish was ignored. The grave is now at Fort Devens, the wish still ignored.

In the fall of 1864 General John S. Marmaduke was brought to Fort Warren, having been captured at Fort Scott on October 24, 1864. Marmaduke graduated from West Point in 1857, and was on duty in New Mexico when the war began. He returned to his home in Missouri, resigned from the army, and raised a company of state guards. Since the policy of the state dissatisfied Marmaduke, he resigned his office there and went to Richmond, where he accepted a commission as first lieutenant under Jefferson Davis, and soon rose to major-general. After the war he was elected governor of Missouri.

Alexander Hamilton Stephens, Vice President of the Confederacy, is the last actor in our Civil War drama. Arrested after he had returned to his home in Crawfordville, Georgia, Stephens was sent to Fort Warren along with Judge Reagan. They reached Boston Harbor at eleven o'clock on the night of May 24, 1865, going ashore the next morning where they were met by Lieutenant William H. Woodman. The group walked around to the old entrance, through the sally port, and descended the stone stairs outside of Quarters Number Seven to the cellar casemates. Stephens was placed in the front room; his door was shut and locked. We read from his journal:

"I was alone, a coal fire was burning; a table and chair were in the centre; a narrow, iron, bunk-like bedstead with mattress and covering was in a corner. The floor was stone—

large square blocks. The door was locked. For the first time in my life I had the full realization of being a prisoner."

Judge Reagan was placed in the next room. We continue with excerpts from Stephens' lengthy journal:

"Sunday—[May 28, 1865]. The horrors of imprisonment, close confinement, no one to see or talk to, with the reflection of being cut off I know not how long—perhaps forever —from communication with dear ones at home, are beyond description. Words utterly fail to express the soul's anguish. This day I wept bitterly. Nerves and spirit utterly forsook me. Yet Thy will be done.

"June 5. Thunder and lightning after candles were out. First thunder since I left Hampton Roads. The warmest night since I have been here. Rose after a refreshing sleep. As has been my custom for many years on arising at home, I commenced singing, in my way, whatever happened to occur to me. This morning I began Moore's hymn:

> *This world is all a fleeting show*
> *For man's illusion given;*
> *The smiles of joy, the tears of woe,*
> *Deceitful shine, deceitful flow—*
> *There's nothing true but Heaven!*

"June 11. 7 p.m. From the parapet on the eastern bastion had a magnificent view of the ocean; as far as the eye could reach, its wide green plain stretched out, placid as the bosom of a lake. I thought of my first view of the great deep, on the 2d of March, 1833. Where I stood this evening is a favorable point for a sea-view; 70 feet above high-water mark, enabling one to look much further out than from any place I have ever been before. On the N.W. bastion got a full, clear outline of Boston, Bunker Hill Monument, etc. Walked out at 6.15. Saw Jackson and DuBose on the opposite bastion—too far to recognize them. Lieut. W. told me who they were. Saw General Ewell on his crutches. He was walking on parapet. I remarked that I thought Ewell had an artificial leg; wondered he did not use it. Lieut. W. replied that Ewell said he was waiting before getting an artificial leg to see if the authorities were going to hang him; if he was going to be hung, he did not care to go to the expense; intended to wait and make out on his crutches until that matter was settled. Ewell has a sense of humour.

"We heard a cannon. Turning toward the point from which the sound came, we saw smoke near a small craft lying at the wharf of a little town, called Hull, nearby. Lieut. W. said, 'Oh, it's Dexter Follet's yacht.' 'Who is he?' asked I. 'A young man of Boston, son of a rich father. He keeps this yacht to sail about as he likes. Carries a gun on board, and always fires it off upon landing or leaving, upon heaving or hoisting anchor.' We saw the yacht on its way to Boston.

"July 5. 3 p.m. The firing of a salute indicates some notable visitor. Two officers stopped opposite my window and looked down upon me. 6.15. Took usual walk. Lieut. W. informed me that salute was in honour of General Robert Anderson and Rear-Admiral Farragut who visited the Fort with a party.

"July 25. If I remain here much longer I shall be bedridden. A little girl brought me some flowers: she got the guard to hold her up, and gave them to me between the bars.

"July 29. Dr. Seaverns entered my room, and announced that he had just got an order authorizing my release from close confinement. The boat had come while I was writing, bringing the mail and with it the order. By it I am allowed to go in and out at pleasure, and walk the grounds when I choose, between sunrise and sunset. In other words I am simply put on parole in the Fort. Lieut. Newton immediately took the lock off my door.

"August 8. A real prison sketch.

Prisoner: What pretty flowers! Let me see them.

Child (*handing them*): They are for you.

Prisoner: Ah! What is your name?

Child: Mabel Appleton.

Prisoner: Oh! It was you who brought me the flowers the other day! Those in the window—wasn't it you?

Mabel: Yes; and they are not faded yet."

F. Lauriston Bullard, chief editorial writer of the *Boston Herald*, corresponded with this little girl Mabel sixty years later, in 1925. She was then about sixty-three years of age but still remembered vividly the scene which Stephens set down on the eighth of August, 1865. After many months of tireless effort, Mr. Bullard had located her through her brother, who was then living in Cincinnati. She wrote Mr. Bullard that she would never forget the occasion when it was her happy privilege to give flowers to the Confederate Vice President.

"Friday, Sept. 1. 7 p.m. Alone in the twilight. What emotions have I experienced since my last entry! Linton [his brother] came by the morning boat.

"October 12. Dr. Seaverns appeared and stated that orders had come for my release. It embraced Judge Reagan and myself.

"October 13. I rose early and now make this last entry. I expect to start by this evening's boat for my dear home. It is a long and hazardous trip for me, beset with many dangers. But, O God deliver me from all evil."

We step ahead to the year 1895. As we land at the dock, we notice several soldiers fishing, and one of them has a sizable pile of fish for his evening meal. Three fine buildings have been erected on the right of the walk leading up to the postern gate, and on inquiry we find they were built because of complaints of officers forced to live inside the damp casemates. A track for construction materials runs up to the eastern rampart, but the work here has been temporarily abandoned. As we walk up the wooden planking, we notice that a new entrance, not quite six feet high, has been cut into the northwestern bastion. This entrance, called the postern gate, was made by widening a carronade embrasure. The postern gate opens into a pretty little enclosure flanked by the inside walls of the bastion, the casemates of which are occupied by the hospital and the doctor's quarters. The hospital is in the same location it was in 1864 when young McBlair dropped into the moat in his attempt to escape. The slate walks of the enclosure are bordered by pretty flowers, and shade is given by maple and horse-chestnut trees. The children of this 1895 fort pass us on their way to school in the city, and the boat whistles impatiently for them to hurry. Squads of soldiers are drilling on the parade ground, and the sharp commands of the officers echo in the morning air.

In one of the casemates a theater has been made, complete with stage, drop-curtain, and scenery, where divers types of drama are presented. A typical play of the "gay nineties," *A Box of Monkeys,* was given here a few weeks before. Other quarters located near the hospital are the Post Exchange, the blacksmith shop, and the tailor shop. Out on the parade ground a group of men are constructing a new portcullis.

One hundred and fifty soldiers are garrisoned at the fort

in this year of 1895, and are commanded by Major William Sinclair of the 2nd Artillery, who came here in 1889 from Alabama. Major Sinclair was formerly a commander under General Sherman. But our time is growing short, so after reviewing again the many interesting places at the island, we go down to the pier and board the boat for our homeward journey. Thus ends our visit to the Fort Warren of the "eighteen-nineties."

Colonel Sinclair left the island in September 1895, and Major Carle A. Woodruff arrived from Fort Adams to take his place, bringing Batteries M and C with him.

Woodruff was still in command when the Spanish War broke out, and Fort Warren again assumed an important role. The Spanish fleet was hourly expected near Boston, and Massachusetts was again caught unprepared. There were but three batteries on duty guarding the entire Massachusetts coastline, and they were all in Boston Harbor. Two were at Fort Warren and one was at Long Island Head. In 1896, it was agreed that 175 breech-loading rifles and mortars were to be set up within ten years. Not only was this plan not carried out, but two years later when the war came only twenty-four pieces were actually mounted. In addition there were less than 250 officers and men stationed at the Boston Harbor batteries.

To help the defense, the 1st Regiment of Massachusetts Artillery was ordered out on April 25, 1898, and in less than twenty-four hours was marching to Rowe's Wharf where the men embarked on the *General Lincoln* for Fort Warren. Plans had been made to quarter the men in portable barracks sent down to the island, but when the regiment arrived it was found that the Deer Island prisoners engaged in setting up the barracks were not very far along in their work. The entire regiment took over the task, and before dark the combined efforts of soldiers and prisoners, who were soon christened the 3rd Corps Cadets, succeeded in erecting enough barracks for the night. The soldiers then had a new rhyme to put to an old song:

> *They broke our backs*
> *A-lugging shacks*
> *In the regular army-O!*

A huge mess-tent was erected, which was very pretty to look at in good weather but sagged miserably in the rainy season which soon came. One day it collapsed into the mud, and the men were forced to seek the "Dark Arch" or the casemated gymnasium facing Bug and Boston Lights. The officers' quarters, located on each side of the massive sally port, were soon crowded. Lieutenant-Colonel Charles B. Woodman, Surgeon Dearing, Major Dyar, Major Quinby, and Major Frye occupied one room which was lighted by three musketry loopholes and looked out on the dry moat and the northern cover face. But according to Major Frye, the room "had an open grate in which a coal fire was always glowing, and on the nights when the rain drove down upon the muddy parade, or when the impenetrable fog swept over the ramparts it was far from lacking in comfort." The enlisted men were quartered fifteen in a shack.

On the twenty-ninth of April, 1898, the regiment changed from the Massachusetts Volunteer Militia to the United States Volunteers, with Major Carle A. Woodruff, still the commanding officer at Fort Warren, mustering the men into service.

Now began the period of rumors. Not only did the reports of the Spanish fleet persist in New England, but on the night of April 26 there was a public banquet in Havana to celebrate the bombardment of Boston. It was known that the Spanish flotilla had left the Cape de Verde Islands on the twenty-ninth of April for an unknown destination. A careful record of all the rumors was kept by an officer at the fort and it is a weird collection. On one occasion, an observer watching in the gathering dusk sighted four ships in single file and believed them to be the Spanish fleet coming to destroy Boston. It turned out to be merely an innocent tug with three barges in tow!

On September 2 the men lined the parapets and cheered the returning fleet of nine warships as it steamed into Boston Harbor. The 3rd Battalion paraded as escort to the men of the fleet in Boston the next day. But the days of war activity were drawing to a close, and the final review was held September 17, 1898. Commander Woodruff saw the soldiers off at the dock, and as they boarded the *City of Philadelphia*, he complimented the battalion on its discipline and efficiency.

After the Spanish War, affairs at Fort Warren settled down to routine assignments until 1900, when barracks were constructed on the northwestern shore.

The last prisoner to be incarcerated in the demilune from which Sawyer escaped in 1863 was a buck private who was confined in 1901. This soldier set fire to his bunk when he was in a rage. After the blaze was put out he was taken to another section of the fort.

During the First World War the old quarters were again crowded with troops, and scores of tents were placed all over the island. About sixteen hundred men were quartered at Fort Warren during the winter of 1917, mostly from the 55th Artillery. The 55th Artillery Regiment was made up of eight companies from Boston and vicinity and came into being in December 1917. Many Coast Artillery units in and around Boston aided in building the 55th up to the needed regimental strength. The Boston Fusiliers, the Famous Tiger Battalion of *John Brown* fame, and the Washington Light Guards were some of the well-known units that were assimilated in filling out the 55th.

On March 8, 1918, came the first news that the men were soon to leave for the front. The notification was in the form of a scarlet fever quarantine, but the troops guessed the real significance of the quarantine—to keep them at the island until called for the trip to France. The expected orders came on March 15, and the 55th Regiment of Coast Artillery left Fort Warren for New York and the *Mauretania*.

The soldiers who later came to Fort Warren as replacements for the 55th tell the story of the attempted murder of a captain while he was stationed at Fort Warren. As far as can be ascertained the incident occurred in the spring of 1918 when replacements for the 55th were training at the island. A private who had grown to hate his captain planned a terrible death for the officer. Every day he watched the captain come up the walk, go through the postern gate, and walk out on the parade ground. He gradually evolved the plan of dropping a heavy cannon ball, a relic of the war of 1861, on the head of the officer just as the captain stepped onto the slate walk of the parade ground.

The time for the attempt at murder came, and the captain started up the walk. The private hidden on the terreplein high above the doorway had the cannon ball in readiness. The officer went through the postern gate and was about to come out onto the parade ground when the cannon ball crashed on the slate walk at his feet. Fortunately the private miscalculated and dropped the fifty-pound ball too soon. Instead of crushing the captain's head, it cracked the slate walk into several pieces. When apprehended, the private claimed innocence; he had so timed his movements that no serious charge could ever be proved against him. The cracks in the walk can be seen today.

Modern warfare was so changed by 1928 that it was decided to reduce grand old Fort Warren to a caretaking status, and the fort was decommissioned late in the summer of that year. The 13th Infantry, then at the island, was sent to Fort Ethan Allen. Sergeant James F. Ward, James Moriarty of the Quartermaster Corps, with Privates Barrito and Green made up the lonely foursome that remained at Fort Warren. A short time later Ward met his death in a tragic accident. A fine likeness of the sergeant was sketched in one of the cellar casemates.

On the ninth of June, 1935, many patriotic and historical societies met at Fort Warren to dedicate a tablet honoring three of the Southern notables who had been imprisoned at George's Island during the era of the Civil War. The men so honored were James Murray Mason, John Slidell, and Alexander Hamilton Stephens. President-General Mrs. W. E. Massie of Hot Springs, Arkansas, spoke for the United Daughters of the Confederacy and the South. Confederate Veteran William B. Newell took the long journey from Richmond, Virginia, to represent the survivors of Lee's armies. Commander Charles L. Robinson, ninety-three, represented the Grand Army of the Republic. Francis DeCelles, representing the Governor of Massachusetts and the North, spoke very effectively. President Mrs. Albert L. Rider of the Boston Chapter, U.D.C., added much to the ceremony with her words of welcome, while Mrs. Roscoe H. Chesley, President of the Woodrow Wilson Chapter, U.D.C., gave a fine reading of *The Blue and the Gray*. The most impressive part of the ceremony, however, was when the two men, the Blue and the Gray, met and shook hands beneath the tablet. It was a very touching scene as they stood with clasped hands in the crowded casemate of Quarters Number Seven, probably the last time two representatives of the North and South will ever meet at Fort Warren.

A letter from President Franklin D. Roosevelt was read at the Fort Warren exercises. It said in part that "we have heard the last mutterings of the storm that more than seventy years ago swept over this country. The people of our land are now completely united in their devotion to the Republic."

An unexpected thrill was given the gathering which had crowded into the casemates of Quarters Number Seven when Commander Robinson told of meeting and shaking the hands of a veteran of the Battle of Bunker Hill of 1775. The Bunker Hill veteran had been about one hundred years old, while Robinson was a very small boy. Thus the lives of these two men spanned the entire life of our nation. It was very fitting that Robinson, speaking at the Fort named after Joseph Warren, should have mentioned that he had shaken the hand of a comrade of Warren. Warren himself was killed at the Battle of Bunker Hill.

During the Second World War units of the 9th and 241st were active at Fort Warren, and after their training they were sent all over the world. I recall meeting veterans from Fort Warren both in England and in the Mediterranean. Some were taken prisoner by the Japanese, while others are buried in the roadside cemeteries overlooking beautiful Oran in North Africa, where I was a convalescent for several weeks in 1942.

In 1957 the General Services Administration decided to sell or dispose of many of the islands in Boston Harbor under their control. I attended the auction of Fort Warren and inadvertently made a bid for the island at about $10,000.

Luckily the bidding went higher, and the island was sold to a group interested in using the deep dungeons and passages for the storage of contaminated atomic material. Because of this turn of events, a group of us decided to make an attempt to retain the island for Massachusetts, and I was elected the president of the Society for the Preservation of Fort Warren.

After many interviews and group meetings, the Metropolitan District Commission agreed to ask the General Services Administration for the island. That part of the arrangement was satisfactory, but unfortunately or fortunately as the case may be, the GSA not only gave the MDC the island, but included with the gift Lovell's Island in which the MDC was not too interested. As I write these words Lovell's Island is still deserted and has become more or less of a problem for the MDC.

Fort Warren, however, is a different matter. After weeks and then months of preparation, the island was officially opened in the summer of 1961. At the opening day speech which I made as president of the Society for the Preservation of Fort Warren, I stressed the hope that the island would be open for students and scholars as well as for yachtsmen.

One of the most important services ever held at Fort Warren took place on Friday, May 24, 1963, when a massive stone slab honoring the Southern heroes who died while prisoners at this Northern bastille was dedicated. Among those who spoke were Mrs. Harold C. Hart, the Rev. Ernest R. Case, Miss Dorothy Snow, Mrs. Webster A. Kefauver, Milton Cook, Mrs. Robert Bachman, Right Rev. Monsignor Joseph Lyons, and Mrs. E. Winslow Ware. This fine memorial marker can be seen by any craft approaching the fort from the west and also by airplanes flying over or near George's Island, where Fort Warren stands.

Every island has its legends, but perhaps the most famous of them all concerns the Lady in Black at Fort Warren.

The legend of this famous Lady in Black has been whispered at Fort Warren for many, many years, until now there are quite a few who believe in the existence of this lady of the black robes. I herewith offer the reader the legend without the slightest guarantee that any part of it is true.

During the War Between the States, hundreds of prisoners were captured by Burnside at Roanoke Island. Among the group incarcerated at Fort Warren in the corridor of dungeons was a young lieutenant who had been married only a few weeks before. He succeeded in getting a message to his young wife by the underground railroad, giving complete directions as to where he was and how she could reach him. Being very much in love, she obtained passage on a small sloop, and landed in Hull a few weeks later. She quickly located the home of a Southerner in that town and was fitted out with a pistol and dressed in men's clothing.

Choosing a dark, rainy night, the lady rowed across Nantasket Road and finally landed on the beach at George's Island. Slipping noiselessly by the sentries, she reached the ditch under the Corridor of Dungeons. After giving a prearranged signal, she was hoisted up to the carronade embrasure and pulled through the opening. As soon as husband and wife had exchanged greetings, they made plans for the future. The prisoners decided to dig their way out of the dungeon into the parade ground and immediately set to work. Unfortunately for their plans, a slight miscalculation brought their tunnel within hearing of Northern soldiers stationed on the other side of the wall. Colonel Dimmick was notified and the whole scheme was quickly exposed. The brave little woman, when cornered, attempted to fire at the colonel, but the gun was of the old fashioned pepperbox type and exploded, killing her husband.

Colonel Dimmick had no alternative but to sentence her to hang as a spy. She made one last request—that she be hanged in women's clothing. After a search of the fort, some robes were found which had been worn by one of the soldiers during an entertaniment, and the plucky girl went to her death wearing these robes.

At various times through the years the ghost of the Lady in Black has returned to haunt the men quartered at the fort. On one occasion three of the soldiers were walking under the great arched sally port at the entrance to the fort, and there before them, in the fresh snow, were five impressions of a girl's shoe leading nowhere and coming from nowhere. Later a certain sergeant from Fort Banks was climbing to the top of the ladder which leads to the Corridor of Dungeons when he heard a voice warning him, saying: "Don't come in here!" Needless to say, he did not venture further.

There actually are on record court-martial cases of men who have shot at ghost-like figures while on sentry duty, and one poor man deserted his post, claiming he had been chased by the lady of the black robes.

For many years the traditional poker game was enjoyed in the old ordnance storeroom, and at ten o'clock one night a stone was rolled the entire length of the storeroom. As all the men on the island were playing poker, no explanation could be found. When the same thing happened the next time the men played poker in the evening, the group at the card table decreased appreciably. By the end of the month the ordnance storeroom was deserted, and since that time, if any of the enlisted men wish to indulge in this pastime, they choose another part of the island. The ghost of the Lady in Black was of course blamed for the trouble. Incidentally, there are half a dozen versions of the legend.

Colonel F. J. Parker's description of the Fort Warren of two generations ago is the best ever written on the famous five-bastioned fortification. I offer you a paragraph.

"To one who thoroughly explored the island there will recur vivid reminiscences of the mysterious castles of romance and history. He will find there a sally port, a postern, a draw bridge, and a portcullis. Here, too, are passages under ground and in the walls: turret staircases, huge vaulted apartments, and safe and dark dungeons, the ways to and through which may be set down upon the plans of the engineer corps, but are familiar to no living man. One can be easily bewildered among the crooks and turns, the ups and downs of the corridors, and it needs only a dark and windy night to make almost real the romantic descriptions of the Castle of Udolfo, with its clanging sounds of chains, it sweeping gusts of air, its strange moanings and howlings, and the startling noise of some sudden clang of a shutting door reverberating through the arches."

Fort Warren is an ideal place to spend a summer day. Patriotic societies, students, scholars, and visiting yachtsmen all become enchanted by the ancient citadel. Even those who have claimed history has little attraction for them have fallen under the spell of the fort named for Joseph Warren, the man who fell at Bunker Hill.

There are many points of interest you should visit. The Corridor of Dungeons, the Wallace Warfield Quarters, the beautiful murals in the Chapel where the song "John Brown's Body" was written, the cracked sidewalk where the cannonball fell, the great sally port with its legend "Fort Warren 1850," and the Museum are six places no one should miss. MDC Officer Joseph Boudreau is the historian of Fort Warren. The musketry embrasure where Sawyer squeezed his way to freedom, the bastion where the six naval prisoners escaped, and the dark arch are worthy of your attention. The front room of Quarters Number Seven, where Mason, Slidell, and Stephens were imprisoned, has become a shrine for Southerners, and is the ninth and final point of interest.

And so we say farewell to Fort Warren. Not one person of the thousands who were at George's Island during the Civil War is now living, but their descendants, both in the North and South, should always keep fresh the thoughts of the men who were here during that war. Fort Warren itself is a splendid memorial to them, and should be preserved as an everlasting tribute to those who fought in the conflict of 1861.

2

BOSTON LIGHT

Lighthouses and beacons have always been a fascination to the traveler and sailor, as well as a very necessary part of navigation itself.

An early mention of a lighthouse in American history occurs in Clough's *New England Almanack* for 1701, where the question is asked:

"Whether or no a Light-House at Alderton's point may not be of great benefit to Mariners coming on these Coasts?"

Shurtleff tells us there is no doubt that a beacon and watch house were built there in the early settlement of the colony, and in the Massachusetts Archives at the State House we read that the Town of Hull presented a bill for work done at the beacon. Nothing was actually done to give Boston Harbor a lighted beacon until the first Saturday in January 1713, when John George, Jr., whose father was killed aboard the *Rose*, headed a petition for the erection of a lighthouse.

From a maritime point of view, Boston was the center of the most prosperous and important of all the American colonies in the early eighteenth century. Many of her merchants and shipowners had followed the sea when younger and were willing and anxious that the port be properly protected. Just how progressive these merchants were can easily be seen when we realize that almost half a century elapsed after Boston Light was built before the citizens of New York erected a lighthouse.

On November 5, 1714, the General Court passed an order to the effect that "a Light-House be Erected at the Charge of this Province at the Entrance of the Harbor of Boston on the same Place & Rates proposed in Bill."

On the twenty-fifth of June, 1716, the work was so far advanced that the committee, in looking for a good man to take care of the Light, believed the position worth the equivalent of five dollars a week. George Worthylake, whose father had been a resident of George's Island for many years, was now appointed the first keeper of the first lighthouse in America. His yearly salary of fify pounds was considerably augmented by his income as one of the Boston Harbor pilots.

Worthylake, keeper of Boston Light, petitioned for an increase in salary in 1717. The winter of 1716-1717 had been so stormy it had prevented him from watching his sheep at Greater Brewster. Fifty-nine of them strayed down to the end of the long bar and drowned, and he was paid for the tragedy.

The keeper with his wife, daughter, and two others were drowned off the light in November of the next year when a gale blew up. This unfortunate accident caused the famous lighthouse ballad of Benjamin Franklin to be written. Thirteen years of age at the time, Franklin sold the ballad on the streets of Boston, naming his effort "The Lighthouse Tragedy." As the event had made quite an impression on the

people of Boston, Franklin did a fair business with his first
literary offering, but he tells us in his *Autobiography* that it
was "wretched stuff." Not a single copy is now in existence.
The unfortunate Worthylake family was buried at Copp's
Hill, where the headstone can easily be found near the tool
shed.

Mr. Robert Saunders, who is mentioned as a sloop captain
in 1711, was now ordered to go to "Beacon Island and take
care of the Lighthouse." Within a few days he also perished
in the ocean, and Boston Light gained the doubtful reputation of losing its first two keepers by drowning.

The merchants of Boston now recommended Captain
John Hayes, an experienced mariner, for the position of
keeper of the Light, and he was appointed by the Court on
November 18, 1718. The duties of the keeper were many
and varied at this period in the history of Boston Harbor.
He was health officer, pilot for vessels coming in and going
out of Boston Harbor, custodian of the fog gun, and keeper
of the Light.

John Hayes, called by the late Rufus Candage "an able-
bodied and discreet person," received at first fifty pounds
a year, but when he petitioned for an increase in salary, the
Court raised his annual pay to seventy pounds. In his petition he mentions the habit of entertaining mariners on the
island to make a little extra money for himself, but says that
he "has found the same prejudicial to himself, as well as the
Town of Boston, and therefore has left off giving Entertainment."

On June 29, 1719, Hayes asked for a gallery to be built
on the seaside of the lighthouse so that he could "come to
the Glass to clear off the Ice & Snow in the Winter Time,
whereby the Said Light is much obscured." He also asked,
"That a great Gun may be placed on the Said Island to

answer Ships in a Fogg." The Court took steps to prevent ice from forming on the glass of the light, and also sent a cannon to Little Brewster Island. The cannon is now at Coast Guard headquarters in Connecticut.

On January 13, 1720, a bad fire broke out at Boston Light, caused "by the Lamps dropping on ye wooden Benches & snuff falling off & setting fire."

Two years later Hayes had a hard time inspecting all the ships from plague-ridden European ports, and in this manner lost many piloting jobs. The Court granted him twenty pounds to repay him for the money lost.

The "Great Storm of 1723" did considerable damage to Boston Light. This gale, perhaps the most severe in the eighteenth century, raised a tide estimated at sixteen feet.

The infirmities of age finally forced Hayes to retire from active service, and on August 22, 1733, he notified the government he would leave the service when his year was up.

The merchants of Boston now petitioned for the appointment of Robert Ball, who became the next keeper of Boston Light. Once firmly established at Little Brewster, Ball made a careful survey of the piloting business in Boston Harbor, becoming quite upset upon realizing that other sailing craft in the Harbor were taking his business away from him. He soon petitioned the General Court for the right to have preference, as the others never worked in the winter while his was a year-round task. The other pilots decoyed the masters of ships coming into the Harbor by "wearing a wide vane such as properly belongs to the province boat, and of the same color and livery." The Court gave Ball permission to be the "established pilot" of the Harbor for the next three years, and allowed him to keep two well-fitted boats, unmistakably distinguished. It further decreed that any person who painted his boat with a similar vane would be fined five pounds, the fine to be given to Ball.

Because of the war scare of 1745, a committee went down the Harbor to take measurements for the sinking of hulks in the channel. They landed at Boston Light, and the hospitable keeper at Little Brewster Island entertained them in a manner which John Hayes had long ago decided was unbecoming the keeper of Boston Light. The bill for hospitality to the committee, fifty shillings, was promptly sent up to Boston.

Three years later Ball wrote up to Boston that the lighthouse needed a fresh coat of white paint, and that the building was sadly in need of renovation. The paint was applied, but in 1751 a bad fire damaged the lighthouse, so only the walls remained. A temporary light was now shown from a spar some distance from the remains of the lighthouse. The Light was repaired at a cost of £1170, and, as the Court believed that "the Charge of such repairs should be bourne by those who receive the immediate benefit thereof," a higher duty was instituted.

Captain Ball usually had a servant at the Light, and some years ago I read in the abandoned graveyard at Rainsford Island the following inscription:

HERE LIES YE BODY OF
SAMSON
LATE SERVANT OF
MR. ROBERT BALLS
WHO DIED JUNE 25TH
1762
AGED 60 YEARS

In February 1774 Ball petitioned for his final pay and retired soon after.

Early in July 1775, the Provincial Congress wished to have the lamp and the oil removed, as the Harbor was then blocked up and the establishment at the island useless. On the twentieth of July, Major Vose, leading a small detachment of American troops, visited Boston Light, where the men burned the wooden parts of the lighthouse. On their way back from Little Brewster Island they were met by an armed British schooner, but they outmaneuvered the English ship and reached the mainland. An eye witness, quoted by Frothingham in his *Siege of Boston*, says that he saw "the flames of the light house ascending up to Heaven, like grateful incense, and the ships wasting their powder." The Americans had already cut a thousand bushels of grain in Hull, and now returned safely through the American lines with all their spoils.

The British began at once to repair the lighthouse, and the workmen as they labored were guarded by British marines. But the Americans were not ones to allow the rebuilding to continue, so Washington placed Major Tupper in charge of three hundred men who, on July 31, started from Dorchester and Squantum for Boston Light. They were successful in landing their armed whaleboats at Little Brewster Island, and the historic Battle of Boston Light began. A writer of the period tells us that:

> *When Tupper and his men had landed there*
> *Their enemies to fight them did prepair*
> *But all in vain they could not them withstand*
> *But fell as victims to our valient band.*

The guard defeated, Tupper destroyed the work done on the lighthouse and prepared to leave the island. The tide, however, had gone out and his whaleboats were left stranded there. In the meantime, the British had sent their own small boats to the island, and as the Americans finally pushed their boats into deep water, they were attacked by the English troops.

The Americans were helped in this new skirmish by a field piece under the command of Major Crane at Nantasket Head. When the situation looked threatening to the Yankees trying to leave the island, a direct shot from the American gun crashing into one of the English boats turned the tide of battle. After the British retired to their boats, it was found that only one American had been killed, while the English losses were comparatively heavy. Major Tupper brought a badly wounded British soldier to Hull, where he soon died. His gravestone is still pointed out by the older inhabitants of Hull, the more historical of whom will tell you that Susanna Rowson herself led the services at his funeral.

George Washington was so pleased with the work of Major Tupper that he commended the major and his men for their "gallant and soldier-like behavior in possessing themselves of the enemie's post at the lighthouse."

After the British left Boston on March 17, 1776, they lingered down the Harbor menacing all the towns of the bay. Samuel Adams was quite indignant that nothing was done to make the British leave the Harbor and suggested in a letter that the various islands be fortified. Tudor tells us in his diary that eight ships, two snows, two brigs, and a schooner still remained in the Harbor. On June 13, 1776, American soldiers landed on Long Island and at Nantasket Hill; the next day they opened fire on the fleet and soon had the English ships at their mercy. The British vessels weighed anchor and sailed down the Harbor, but they sent a boat ashore at Boston Light, leaving a time charge which blew up the lighthouse, thus repaying the Americans who had twice damaged the Light under British rule.

A guard of Americans landed at Little Brewster Island shortly after the Light was blown up and recovered much useful material from the debris. The lower part of the tower was still intact. The Council met in Boston on September 3, and decreed that "as the top of the old lighthouse was unfit for further use, it should be delivered to the committee to supply the cannon with ladles."

John Hancock, the Governor of Massachusets, notified the Legislature on November 8, 1780, that no light existed at the entrance to Boston Harbor. The Boston Marine Society addressed a message to the Senate and the House of Representatives, and pointed out that Boston was without a lighthouse to guide shipping to its wharves, and that such a serious defect would have to be remedied before the people of Boston could expect a return of the days of good shipping. The very next month the Commissary-General of Massachusetts was directed to erect a lighthouse on the site of the old structure. The sum granted by the legislature, £1000, lasted until the lighthouse was nearly completed, when an additional £450 was appropriated to finish the job.

The rebuilt lighthouse measured seventy-five feet high, with the walls at the base seven and a half feet thick, tapering to two feet six inches at the top. The lantern, fifteen feet high, was of octagonal shape, and its diameter was approximately eight feet. Keeper Thomas Knox was appointed on November 28, 1783.

The famous vessel *United States,* made her final voyage in 1784. The last entry in her log book, dated May 26, 1784, reads as follows: "Got Thomas Knox, a pilot, on board, just without the lighthouse, and at 3 1/2 got along Mr. Hancock's wharf at Boston. All well." An interested observer when Thomas Knox climbed aboard the United States was Madame Hayley, the sister of John Wilkes of "Wilkes and Liberty" fame.

Boston Light was ceded to the United States Government on June 10, 1790, along with twelve other lighthouses in the country. Massachusetts led the other states by transferring five lighthouses to the national government. Maine, New Jersey, Delaware, Connecticut, Georgia, Rhode Island, South Carolina, and New Hampshire were the other states having a lighthouse located in their territory. There was considerable rivalry between the state and the national governments at this time, and because Knox accepted the position as keeper of Boston Light under the Federal Government he lost his job as "branch pilot" of Boston Harbor.

Pemberton wrote his account of the islands of Boston Harbor about this time, and he mentions Lighthouse Island as follows:

"The Lighthouse on it is sixty-five feet in height. Three branch pilots for the port of Boston attend the island. Their district is from the high lands of Marshfield on the south, to Nahant Rock on the north."

Thomas Knox continued in the service of the Lighthouse Department until 1811, when he was succeeded by Jonathan Bruce. The new keeper brought his wife Mary to live at the lighthouse. The couple witnessed the thrilling encounter between the *Chesapeake* and the *Shannon* on June 1, 1813, the battle lasting but fifteen minutes. The well-trained crew of the English ship *Shannon* made short work of the American ship as the first six minutes practically decided the battle. Captain Lawrence of the *Chesapeake* was carried below, mortally wounded, and as he was lowered through the companionway he cried out to his men, "Don't give up the ship." As the deck of his boat was becoming a shambles, Lawrence's crew obeyed for only nine minutes, when they were forced to surrender the *Chesapeake* to Commander Broke of the English vessel.

Jonathan Bruce and his wife stayed on at the Light after

the war ended. The importance of his position as keeper of Boston Light was somewhat dimmed by the establishment of Long Island Light in 1819. In the spring of the same year, the rambling rhymester of Boston Harbor, Frederick W. A . S. Brown, wrote the following verse in honor of Keeper Bruce:

> *To Bruce, who kindles, when the night*
> *Succeeds the lightsome day;*
> *The slow, revolving, brilliant light,*
> *Now muse, thy tribute pay.*

Jonathan Bruce completed twenty-two years of service at Boston Light in 1833, and then retired to live at Rainsford's Island. His wife, Mary Bruce, died at Elder Rainsford's old home in 1851, and the inscription on her gravestone, which I read in 1935 at Rainsford's Island, is worthy of a place here:

> *Bright be the place of thy soul*
> *No lovelier spirit than thine*
> *E'er barred from its mortal control*
> *In the orbs of the blessed to shine*

Bruce lived until 1868, dying in Boston at the age of seventy-six.

David Tower was the next keeper at Boston Light. The great December hurricanes of 1839, occurring on December 15, 21, and 27, threw more than a score of vessels onto the shores around Boston Harbor, but Tower was helpless to aid the crews of the schooner *Charlotte* and the bark *Lloyd* driven ashore at Nantasket. Less than five years after the triple hurricanes of 1839, David Tower died in service at Boston Light.

Joshua Snow became keeper on October 8, 1844. In that year many fine improvements inside the Light were made.

The lighthouse was equipped with a cast-iron circular stairway, having a central iron pipe and a wrought-iron railing. "A cast iron deck and scuttle were put in, with iron window frames, a large outside door of iron, and an inside door with frame and large arch piece over it." The improvements of 1844 can be seen today, except where repairs have been made.

Captain Tobias Cook of Cohasset relieved Snow in the last week of December 1844. While Cook was keeper of Boston Light, James Lloyd Homer, the man who wrote as the "Shade of Alden," paid him a visit. He tells us that the Light was eighty-two feet above the sea and makes the mistake of believing the steps leading up into the light were of stone. There were two wharves on the southwestern side of the island, according to Homer, and anyone steering his boat between the two piers would be sure of a cordial reception. A rather amazing development at Boston Light was the establishment about this time of a "Spanish" cigar factory, with young girls brought from Boston to work at Little Brewster Island. This business, set up to practice a fraud on the good people of the city, was soon broken up, and the girls were sent back to Boston to work under less romantic conditions. Homer comments on the incongruous situation of a Spanish factory at Boston Light.

Tobias Cook resigned as keeper in 1849, and Captain William Long of Charlestown became the new official in charge of the Light, bringing his family, including a daughter, Lucy, out to Little Brewster. Through the kindness of Mrs. Herbert L. Wilber, I have been allowed to read the diary of her grandmother, Lucy Maria Long, which was kept at Boston Light from October 19, 1849, until October 2, 1851. I will quote from this almost priceless relic of Boston Harbor life 120 years ago.

"Monday, October 29.—Pleasant weather, in the forenoon I went in the cutter's boat to carry Antoinette to the Pilot Boat *Hornet*. In the afternoon I went over to the island, on returning saw the body of a man on the bar, supposedly washed from the wreck of the vessel, lost on Minot's Ledge."

At low tide it is possible to walk across the bar from Boston Light to Greater Brewster Island, and from there well along Brewster Spit; this is the route Miss Long took many times. She tells us that a gentleman came out to the Lighthouse on November 10, 1849, to try to induce her to go to Fort Warren to teach the children of the workmen, but she did not accept the offer as she enjoyed the social life of Little Brewster Island too much to leave it. When her father went ashore Lucy lit the great light herself.

We know that two of the pilot boats of the period were the *June* and the *Sylph*, as they often were mentioned at Boston Light by Lucy.

"Monday, Aug. 26.—Pleasant weather, this morning Albert came down in his boat."

The above-mentioned Albert was the Albert Small of the unusual lighthouse romance which culminated in the proposal at the top of the lighthouse. This courtship between Lucy Maria Long and Pilot Albert Small went on for many months, in spite of the scores of other young pilots who made Little Brewster Island the mecca of their leisure hours. Day after day we read of as many as six pilots landing at once to enjoy a social hour or two at the Light.

One afternoon, accompanied by Sarah Godbold, a six-year-old chaperon, Lucy Maria Long and Albert Small went up to the top of Boston Light, presumably to admire the wonderful view from that well-known vantage point. Albert, however, had an important matter which he wished to discuss with Lucy at this time, and believing the little girl would not realize the full implications of what would occur, led Lucy a few feet away and asked her to marry him. Unfortunately for us she did not enter a detailed account of the incident in her diary, but we do know that her answer given at the top of Boston Light was "Yes."

Sarah was burdened with a very large secret for such a little girl. As soon as the three returned to the lightkeeper's house she informed the family of all which had transpired, to the embarrassment of the happy young people, but the parents and the other pilots were quick to come to the rescue of the blushing pair with hearty congratulations. On June 16, 1853, Lucy Maria Long and Albert Small were married. A daughter of this union, Mrs. Carrie Maria Dickey, lived in Middleboro, Massachusetts, and it was through her daughter, Mrs. Wilber, that we learned of this diary of long ago.

In 1851 Captain William Long was succeeded at Boston Light by Zebedee Small, whose pay at the Light at this time was $400 a year. During his regime, the Lighthouse Board of the United States Government was established. Congress had been investigating the conditions in the Lighthouse Department, and in the act which established the Board it made restrictive regulations affecting those merchants furnishing supplies to lighthouses. Certain ship chandlers had been detected in giving concessions to the purchasing agents who supplied the lighthouses with food, and Congress was determined to prevent such manipulations in the future.

Hugh Douglass became the next keeper of Boston Light on June 2, 1853. The only important change while Douglass was at the lighthouse was in the rapidity of the light's revolution. In 1842, I. W. P. Lewis referred to the mechanism which turned the light as the "machine of rotation," and the speed of revolution at that time was three minutes. Elaborate changes were made by 1854 when the speed was increased to one minute thirty seconds.

Douglass was succeeded in 1856 by Moses Barrett, a native of Gloucester. Boston Light was provided with the Fresnal lamp in the third year of Barrett's term and at the same time the tower was raised to its present height of 98 feet. It was now listed as a second-order station, the rating being determined by the inside diameter of the lens. When the Fresnal lamp was lighted on December 20, 1859, the pilots protested that the new Light was inferior to the old one in brilliancy and power.

When the brig *Ewan Crerar* struck on a ledge near the Graves on March 9, 1860, she came off and anchored between Shag Rocks and Outer Brewster, but filled and sank quickly in forty feet of water. The members of the crew were able to row to Boston Light in the snow-storm.

Barrett was at Boston Light until late in 1862, and his last two years spent there were full of adventures. When Fort Sumter was fired on, April 26, 1861, he knew that exciting times were ahead.

The incident which impressed Barrett more than all the events connected with the war occurred on Sunday morning, November 3, 1861, and was the worst marine tragedy in the history of Boston Harbor. The square rigger *Maritana*, 991 tons, had sailed out of Liverpool on the twenty-fifth of September with Captain Williams in command. She ran into heavy seas coming into Massachusetts Bay and approached Boston in a howling southeaster with a blinding snow falling. About one o'clock in the morning she sighted Boston Light and headed for the beacon, which she was never to pass.

Mr. Barrett had noticed the lights of the vessel earlier in

the evening. At twelve midnight she was bearing E.N.E., when she suddenly changed her course and seemed to be running for the Light. At twelve-twenty she burned her torch lights, and by seeing the *Maritana*'s yards, Barrett knew that she was a square rigger. The snow now came so fast that the lights of the ship disappeared, and Barrett prayed that she had slipped by safely and was then making her way into calmer waters. The gale was increasing at a fearful rate, and even at daybreak nothing could be seen beyond three hundred feet. When Barrett went down on the rocks, he found the standard of a ship and realized that something serious had happened.

As it later developed, the *Maritana* had crashed onto Shag Rocks, a short distance away, and the crew and passengers were then fighting for their lives. The sailors had cut the masts away soon after the ship had struck; many made attempts to reach the ledge but the great waves prevented anyone's reaching the shore of the little isle. The vessel now showed signs of breaking up, and the passengers and crew were ordered into the weather chains.

With the lifting of the snow, the anxious inhabitants of Lighthouse Island were able to see the ship stuck fast on Shag Rocks, but they were helpless to launch a boat in the swirling waters. Barrett then attempted to signal across to Hull, but the wind blew with such force that the signal flag was blown to shreds.

About 8:30 the great ship broke in two, and Captain Williams, standing on the quarter-deck at the time, was crushed to death. Seven people floated to Shag Rocks on the top of the pilot house, while five others were successful in swimming to the same ledge. After the hull of the ship had broken in two, fragments of the wreckage started to come ashore on both sides of the island, and the watchers on

Lighthouse Island saw a body in the surf. By afternoon the sea and the storm had quieted appreciably, and Captain Barrett's signal to Hull was acknowledged. The bodies of the unfortunates now started to wash up on the beach, and that of Captain Williams was among the first. At two o'clock Pilot Boat No. 2, the *William Starkey*, sent a dory ashore at Shag Rocks and rescued the survivors of the tragedy. The boat was manned by Captain Samuel James of Hull, a member of the famous lifesaving family.

The next morning the cutter came down to the scene of the disaster, and Captain Barrett assisted in recovering the nude and battered body of a woman at the end of the Spit.

It was not until the following March that the last member of the crew was found and buried at Little Brewster Island. In the spring of 1862 the wife of Captain Williams came down to the island to receive her husband's watch and other keepsakes which the keeper had been saving for her, and sat with her children on the rocks under the lighthouse. She spent hours looking out at Shag Rocks, the ledge which had broken her family apart forever.

Charles E. Blair became keeper of Boston Light on November 20, 1862, and saw the captured crews of the Confederate ships *Tacony* and *Atlanta* on their way to Fort Warren. Six of these prisoners escaped on the night of August 19, 1863, and two of them sailed by the island on their way down to Maine where they were captured. Blair returned to the mainland on July 18, 1864, and was replaced by the celebrated Thomas Bates.

Captain Bates was honored many times for his heroism while in the employ of the Lighthouse Department, and many men still living have told me of his sterling bravery. Wesley Pingree, former keeper at Deer Island Light, related to me the story of the day at Minot's Lighthouse when two men were drowning near the ledge. Bates, alone at the Light, took the dangerous risk of letting himself down in his dory from the top of the light. He reached the men and saved both of them from the raging storm. Bates took charge of another rescue on January 31, 1882, at the time the *Fanny Pike* went ashore on Shag Rocks. She went to pieces quickly, but Captain Bates rowed out to the little ledge and took the crew off safely. Assistant Keeper Bailey and Charles Pochaska, a young fisherman who lived on Middle Brewster Island, helped him make the rescue.

Bates spent many pleasant nights at the lighthouse, and Assistant Keeper Edward Gorham, with his accordion, helped along the musical program which they all enjoyed on Sunday evenings. Bates, admonishing the others to sing louder, would tell Gorham to "bear down" on his accordion as they sang *When the Roll Is Called up Yonder* and *Crossing the Bar*, every sailor's favorite. After almost thirty years of service Thomas Bates died on the island on April 6, 1893.

Alfred Williams assumed charge until the official appointment was made on May 3, 1893, when Albert M. Horte was made keeper of Boston Light. His young sister Josephine played about the island at this time and still remembers when she used to turn cartwheels over the old fog gun that had been brought to the island in 1719. Horte was keeper less than a year, relinquishing his post to Henry L. Pingree, whose son, Wesley, became interested in Albert M. Horte's sister Josephine. Wesley Pingree and Josephine Horte were later married, spending their honeymoon at Deer Island Light.

Early one morning in 1897, as Pingree's son Wesley was walking down to start the fire for the fog signal, he was amazed to see the boat from Portland, Maine, in between Shag Rocks and the Outer Brewster. She backed out without striking, but a glance at a chart will give the reader an idea of the craft's precarious situation.

The terrible storm on November 27, 1898, will probably always be remembered as the "Portland storm," as the Steamship *Portland* then left Boston for the last time. Another ship, the *Calvin F. Baker,* pushed up on Lighthouse Island, so close to the buildings there that when the ship rolled, the people on the island felt as if they could almost reach out to save the sailors. But the crew of the ship was frozen fast to the rigging, and cried out for help all during the next night. The keeper was unable to aid the men until morning, when the survivors were landed. Three sailors were lost from the ship. The terrible screams of the helpless men freezing in the rigging so affected Keeper Pingree's wife that she died shortly afterward.

Henry Pingree's son was made an assistant at Boston Light, and one day he and the other assistant took the lighthouse dory to Fort Warren where they boarded the *Resolute* to go to Boston to get a forty-pound reed for the fog signal. While in town, a terrible storm blew up, and when Pingree and the other assistant returned to Fort Warren they were warned not to attempt to reach Boston Light that afternoon. Believing that the fog signal should be repaired, they started from the dock at Fort Warren in the dory. As the little boat came out from the lee of George's Island, the full force of the gale hit them, and they could not make any progress toward the Light. A mud digger was anchored a few hundred yards away, and the men fought their way to her, tying the dory in the lee of the craft. The captain told them he wouldn't take them to Boston Light that night for a million dollars, so they spent the evening with him. Later that night the dory was washed away, and the reed went with it.

The next morning, during a lull in the storm, the captain of the mud digger had them landed at Bug Light, and at low tide they successfully walked along Greater Brewster Spit and Lighthouse Bar until they reached Boston Light. The soldiers at George's Island had watched and waited for the dory to pass out through the Narrows the previous afternoon, and when it failed to come in sight the men believed the keepers had drowned. When the overturned dory washed up on the beach the next morning, their fears seemingly were confirmed. The Lighthouse Department was notified, and the *Geranium* started for the outer islands. She reached Boston Light, but the storm had so increased by this time that she could do nothing but steam up and down Lighthouse Channel, unable to send a boat ashore. In order to notify the *Geranium*'s captain that all were safe, every man at the Light came outside and joined hands in front of the lighthouse. The captain counted the men, and with a quick whistle of farewell turned his ship around for the trip back to Boston.

Keeper Henry Pingree left Boston Light on November 1, 1909. His successor, Levi B. Clark, witnessed the terrible gale on Christmas Day, 1909, when the five-masted schooner *Davis Palmer* hit on Finn's Ledge and went down with all hands. She was heavily loaded with coal, and the captain, Leroy M. Kowen, had hoped to dock before noon. His wife, living in Malden, had Christmas dinner cooking when she heard the terrible news. Part of the wreckage of the vessel washed ashore at Boston Light. My cousin, John I. Snow of Rockland, Maine, did salvage work on the *Palmer*.

During the week of September 3, 1910, the Squantum Air Meet took place, and Claude Graham-White made his memorable flight to Boston Light from Squantum. Assistant Keeper Jennings waved down to the flyer as the airplane roared by just below the top of the Light. An eye-witness of the event, Dr. William M. Flynn of Dorchester, tells us that there was a line of motor boats and naval launches stretched all the way from Squantum out to the Light, as many thought that Graham-White would surely drop into the water at some point in his trip. The Bostonian Society has a fine collection of pictures taken at the time.

Keeper Levi B. Clark left the Island in 1911, and for a few months George Kezar was keeper of Boston Light. Kezar, who had been at Duxbury Pier in Plymouth, finally retired from the service in June 1935. He had passed many years of activity serving at several of the well-known lights along the coast.

Mills Gunderson became the next man in charge of Little Brewster Island. It was during his regime that the Boston Light Swim gained nation-wide prominence. This grueling endurance test from Charlestown to Boston Light has attracted hundreds of boys and men since its inauguration. Sam Richards is perhaps the best known of all the contestants who successfully negotiated the distance.

Charles H. Jennings was appointed to take charge of the beacon on Little Brewster Island on May 1, 1916, and served during the hectic war days when the U-boat scares alarmed the coast. Before the war began, the two hundredth anniversary of the lighting of the beacon on Little Brewster Island was observed, on September 25, 1916.

Perhaps the most thrilling experience in which Jennings participated was the rescue of the men on the *U.S.S. Alacrity*, which was wrecked on the ice-covered ledges off Lighthouse Island on February 3, 1918, at three forty-five in the morning. Captain Jennings, awakened by the sound of gunfire, aroused the assistant keepers, Lelan Hart and Charles Lyman, who rushed down to the shore. They saw the doomed ship and endeavored to reach it by firing the gun of the Massachusetts Humane Society. Four attempts were made, but each time the rope parted as the shells used were very old. Jennings now brought the dory down to the shore, and, assisted by sailors Hero and Harvey of the Naval Reserves, pushed the dory over the ice and into the surf.

Twenty-four men were clinging to the wreck of the *Alacrity* and their position was precarious. If they fell in between the ice cakes, they could not keep afloat and, if they stayed on the boat, she might soon slip off the ledge and sink. Jennings and his two assistants finally reached the wreck after a perilous trip, flung a line aboard, and began the rescue of the half-frozen sailors. Four times the men ran the gauntlet of ice, rocks, and raging surf until they finally succeeded in saving all twenty-four of the men. For this heroic deed Jennings later received a letter of commendation from William C. Redfield, Secretary of Commerce.

In 1919 Jennings was given the position as keeper of the range lights on Lovell's Island. J. Lelan Hart succeeded Jennings as keeper of Boston Light. Hart's first knowledge of the islands of Boston Harbor was obtained during the shipwreck of his boat loaded with lime at Outer Brewster Island. The vessel was a coaster, *A. Heaton*, owned by A. C. Gay of Rockland, Maine. As the vapor whistle at Boston Light had been out of order, the ship had crashed onto the rocks in a dense fog. The lime caught fire, and Captain Hart's ship burned to the water's edge. Fortunately the captain and members of the crew escaped to safety by rowing to Boston Light in the lifeboats.

Maurice Babcock succeeded Lelan Hart in 1926. Babcock and his wife and family spent many more years at the Light, and his record is a fine one. Our visits to him were many.

Keeper Babcock told us there were only two things of primary importance: one the Light itself, and the other the fog signal. If he was sure that both were in good working order, he was at peace with the world and a happy man. Maurice Babcock and his wife, Mrs. Mary Babcock, had five children, Helen, John, Grace, Hazel, and Maurice Junior. First Assistant Keeper Bickford Haskins had five children, and Second Assistant Keeper Ralph Norwood had eight children. Georgia Faith Norwood was one of the few babies ever born at Boston Light during its many years of activity. The event took place at ten thirty-five on the morning of April 11, 1932.

On the second day of December 1934, a memorial list of the twenty-five keepers of Boston Light was unveiled in the lighthouse itself by Fitz-Henry Smith, Jr. The Coastguard boat *Pueblos,* which took the party out to Lighthouse Island, had previously stopped at Spectacle Island to pick up Keeper Lelan Hart, and had put in at Lovell's Island to allow Keeper Charles Jennings to join the group. A brisk westerly gale had sprung up, and the landing at the Light was completed under difficulty, with many of the party getting a wetting.

On September 14, 1966, the 250th anniversary of Boston Light was observed at the island, with Elliot Richardson the principal speaker. I recited in Greek, Homer's words on the "watch fire's light."

The two dogs, Salty I and later Salty II, were outstanding canines at the island during the last generation.

The keepers at Boston Light since Maurice Babcock have been Ralph C. Norwood, 1941; Franklin A. Goodwin, 1945; Julio Di Furia, 1945; Eldon W. Beal, 1946; Leo F. Gracie, 1946; Stanley Batt, 1948; Joseph F. Lavigne, 1948; John D. Hall, 1950; Robert C. Merchant, 1950; Clinton M.

Davis, 1951; Ray O. Beard, 1951; Robert A. Reedy, 1952; John Curran, 1952; Paul B. Guy, 1953; Hubert B. Jones, 1954; John E. Horner, 1955; J. B. Collins, 1960; G. Schiffers, 1961; W. F. Mikelonis, 1962; V. T. Springer, 1966; Allick Rust, 1969.

I can do no better in closing this chapter on Boston Light than to quote from the gifted pen of Fitz-Henry Smith, Jr. "Boston Light is still a commanding object at the entrance of the Harbor, though it is not so prominent a feature of the landscape as it once was, for its pre-eminence is now disputed by the new and more powerful light on the Graves. Its importance to mariners has been lessened by the opening of the new channel in Broad Sound; but its distinction as the oldest light in the country, and its history, are possessions that can never be taken away."

3

CASTLE ISLAND

A hopeful band of twenty Puritans led by Governor Thomas Dudley sailed across Boston Harbor on the twenty-ninth of July, 1634, and landed at what is now Castle Island, looking for a good site for their proposed fort. The first attempt to plan defenses for the area had ended in failure, and these twenty men were determined to agree on a good location before returning to Boston. They climbed to the top of the cliff and were so impressed with the commanding view its twenty acres offered that they decided Castle Island best suited their needs. Dudley and each man present subscribed five pounds for the fortification, and the group elected Deputy-Governor Roger Ludlow to take charge of the actual construction.

None of the first three commanders of the fort stayed long at the Castle. Nicholas Simpkins, who was given the honor of being the first to command the defense, became involved in financial difficulties within the year, and resigned his position. He was succeeded by Lieutenant Edward Gibbons of Pullen Point, whose many enterprises forced him also to relinquish the office. Richard Morris became the next commander.

It was while Morris was at the Castle that the first tragic incident took place. In the summer of the year 1637 three ships sailed into the Harbor from Ipswich. When the Castle boat ordered the vessels to stop, two of them dropped anchor, but the third sailed by. The gunner at the Castle sent a warning shot across her bow, but the wet powder delayed the firing of the gun just long enough to kill a passenger in the rigging of the vessel. The next day the coroner and a magistrate, after boarding the ship and viewing the dead body, rendered the verdict that the poor man "came to his death by the Providence of God." Probably this decision eased the minds of the good Puritan villagers, but it was of no use to the unfortunate victim.

Affairs in New England were so quiet in 1642 that the General Court decided the Castle was no longer needed for protection, and in May 1643 gave orders to abandon the island. These instructions had hardly been carried out when the colorful La Tour, fresh from his struggles with D'Aulnay, sailed into Boston Harbor. His ship, the *Clement*, carrying 140 people, fired a friendly greeting as it neared the island; but there was no answering gun from the deserted fort. A short distance away La Tour saw a small boat, piloted by a woman. Mrs. Gibbons, wife of the former commander at the Castle, was taking her children down to their farm at Pullen Point. La Tour had a boat lowered and started to overtake them, but she became frightened and made for Governor's Island, where John Winthrop was then living. Governor Winthrop, hearing the cannon shot, had come down to the beach to find out the cause of the disturbance. Mrs. Gibbons was able to land on the shore before La Tour caught up with her. When the Frenchman reached the beach, he explained that it had merely been his intention to ask Mrs. Gibbons a few questions about the settlement at Boston. Meanwhile, the Harbor was filling with boats of all descriptions, manned by loyal colonists who feared their governor was in danger. The citizens were soon reassured by Winthrop and returned to their homes. But Winthrop, writing in his journal, believed that "if La Tour had been ill-minded towards us . . . he might have gone and spoiled Boston." Shortly thereafter, the Castle was refortified.

During the civil war in England there were many engagements in America between the Royalists and those in favor of a parliamentary government. Boston Harbor was the scene of a fierce struggle between two ships manned by these opposing factions, in which the Royalist vessel was forced to surrender. This battle right under the guns of the Castle was too much for Captain Davenport, and he soon forced the victorious ship to surrender its prize. The Court now ordered him to exercise caution in Boston Harbor, advising him to stamp out fighting between ships whenever possible.

Davenport was constantly troubled by money matters, especially in 1654, when the towns were asked to send men and supplies to the Castle to help out with expenses. Boston did what it could by giving the Castle a great bell, and later sent a substantial supply of gun powder.

This bell has an unusual history. One of the few actual treasures from John Winthrop's period, it was probably captured by Spanish pirates from a Scandinavian ship in the early part of the seventeenth century. A little later Captain Thomas Cromwell, commissioned by the Earl of Warwick to go after the pirates, captured at least four of these Spanish ships. Having become a rich man, he settled at Boston in 1646. The Suffolk Records contain his will mentioning six bells which he gave to Boston. The bells were distributed for various purposes, but the one in which we are interested was sent over to Castle Island in 1655 for the use of Captain Davenport. We know that this bell was in continuous service at the island until 1831, but years ago it was turned over to the Bostonian Society by Major Raymond of the Engineering Corps. It was placed on a window ledge at the Old State House, the lettering indicating that it originally belonged to the ship *Patrioten*.

The troubles of Captain Davenport were soon to be ended. One hot day in July 1665, deciding to forget for a time the cares of office, he lay down on his cot beside the powder magazine. A thunderstorm came up and a bolt of lightning struck the room, killing Davenport and injuring several of his men. It was a miracle that the Castle was not blown to pieces, since the magazine was only a few feet away.

A fire in March 1673 destroyed practically all the buildings on the island. Governor Bellingham had just died, and due to the confused state of his will the shrewd colonists voted to use his money for the erection of a new fort, sixty feet square. There were only six men in all at the island to man the thirty guns eventually installed there. The next commander, Roger Clap, was constantly getting into trouble with the General Court, and, if it had not been for his private income, he would have been forced to leave the fort. But when James II sent Sir Edmund Andros to be governor of what was termed the Dominion of New England, Clap took his family and moved off the island. He resigned his position rather than serve under this hated baronet.

When Clap died at the age of eighty-two, he was buried in King's Chapel Burying Ground. Some years ago an ambitious superintendent in charge of burials decided to arrange the gravestones in accordance with the new scheme of pathways he planned for the cemetery. Unmindful that this would destroy the connection between the stones and the actual graves, he rearranged many of the headstones so that they were finally placed far from their original locations. Roger Clap's headstone suffered in this respect, and, although we may go into the Chapel Burying Grounds today and view his tombstone, we must realize it is not over his grave.

In 1691, the new charter decreed that the Lieutenant or Deputy-Governor of the colony should automatically become the commander at Castle Island. Lieutenant-Governor William Stoughton therefore became the new official at the island. Stoughton Hall, at Harvard College from which he graduated in 1650, was named for him. He was the most prominent citizen Dorchester had produced. A distinguished preacher, he was asked to take the place of Rev. Richard Mather when this good man died, but declined. He was chief justice in the court that tried the witchcraft cases, Samuel Sewall being his colleague.

Stoughton noticed the Castle was in a wretched condition, partly due to a disastrous fire twenty years before, and reported it to his superior in England. Nothing was done to repair the crumbling fortress until the turn of the century, with the arrival of Colonel Wolfgang William Romer. This chief military engineer of all the British forces in North America surveyed the situation carefully. He decided the old Castle was beyond repair and ordered it torn down. In 1701 the actual construction of what was to be known as Castle William began.

Samuel Sewall began to hear rumors concerning the vocabulary of this famous builder of North American forts, and rowed over to the island to obtain first hand knowledge. He landed at the Castle and walked up to the fortifications. Sewall noticed the fine construction with pleasure, but on hearing Romer admonishing his workmen he was worried. His loyal Puritanism could not countenance this builder who swore, but he realized the man was a great engineer. After thinking the situation over carefully for a few days, he advised the men to turn a deaf ear to the cursings of Romer, but to listen attentively when he spoke concerning the actual construction of the fort.

With the completion of the fort a most unusual law was passed by the colony. If a man fell in debt, he must stand the risk of serving as a soldier at Castle Island until the amount of the indebtedness had been worked out. If the fort already had a full garrison of soldiers, one man must be discharged to make room for the delinquent citizen.

The European situation had become so alarming by 1708 that it was decided to recruit the Castle to its full strength of eighty soldiers. The treaty of Utrecht was five years away, and Louis XIV was still the most feared monarch in Europe. To help recruiting, the Colony offered a bonus of three pounds to any man who would join the forces at this time.

Three years later the entire Harbor was aroused by news flashed up from Hull that a vast armada was sailing on Boston. By the time the fleet reached the Road, every able-bodied man was armed, and the Castle was alive with excitement. It was an English fleet, fortunately, and Sir Hovendon Walker's squadron of sixty-one ships with five regiments from Marlborough's army soon anchored off the Castle. It was the largest fleet that had ever floated on the waters of Boston Harbor. Walker's squadron remained here a few weeks and then sailed for the disastrous expedition into Canada. The sketching of this grand fleet as it bade adieu to the harbor islands would have made a wonderful subject for some contemporary artist.

William Tailer, who was in charge at this time, noticed a change in the soldiers at the castle. Probably inspired by the battleships in the Harbor, they had developed a new interest in warfare. Many Sunday afternoons the rattle of musketfire could be heard by the good folk of Boston, possibly trying to sit through the second hour of one of Cotton Mather's sermons. Because of the disturbance from the fort, a law was passed forbidding the shooting of guns at the island on the Lord's Day. It is indeed fortunate that some irreligious invader, taking advantage of the Sunday edict, did not sail by the silent fort and capture the town single-handed.

We should pity the poor soldier of this period at the island. Never paid on time, his privileges gradually restricted, life was quite drab and colorless. So evidently thought one Christopher Bagley, a soldier at the fort. Bagley deserted his commander and his wife by turning sailor, leaving Boston as a common able-bodied seaman. His wife Mary waited a while and then asked for the back pay due her husband. She was granted the amount in full, seven pounds, eleven shillings, and four pence.

On October 19, 1716, Lieutenant-Governor William Dummer assumed control at Castle Island, which was now recognized as the most important fort in British North America. John Larrabee, being senior officer, really was more in charge than Dummer, who spent much of his time at his Newbury farm. When the colonial legislature discovered that Dummer had been using three soldiers from the fort to work on his farm at Newbury, and was asking the government to pay for their board, there were many arguments between the executive and legislative branches of

Massachusetts. The most famous of these controversies is recorded as the *Case of the Muster Rolls,* but, although Dummer's accounts were finally accepted, the legislature believed that the circumstances were quite unusual.

The year 1728 brought over William Burnet, son of the Bishop of Salisbury, as the new governor of Massachusetts. Mather Byles thought the occasion was great enough to compose a complimentary poem in Burnet's honor.

When a committee of inspection visited Castle Island in 1736, they found everything but the brickwork in good condition. A new battery was voted, and was erected fifty yards from the fort. In 1740 the guns were carefully mounted. Five years later some of these guns were borrowed and taken by the Massachusetts naval fleet to Louisburg, where they aided in the capture of that famous stronghold.

With the fall of Louisburg, France sent a great squadron against Boston, and one hundred and eleven ships were soon crossing the Atlantic to destroy Massachusetts. Great storms again came to Boston's rescue as the fleet was blown far off its course, and as Longfellow tells us:

> *Like a potter's vessel broke*
> *The great ships of the line,*
> *They were carried away as a smoke,*
> *Or sank like lead in the brine.*
>
> *O Lord! before Thy path*
> *They vanished and ceased to be,*
> *When Thou didst walk in wrath*
> *With thine horses through the sea!*

In 1753 splendid new barracks three hundred and sixty feet long were erected at the island for the troops of Shirley and Pepperell. The regular garrison, of course, was kept in the citadel itself. William Pepperell, the hero of Louisburg, became commander of Castle William in 1757. He was succeeded the same year by Governor Pownall, whose fine sketch of the Castle of that period still exists.

In 1761 Governor Pownall was appointed to South Carolina, Governor Francis Bernard of New Jersey succeeding him in Massachusetts. Bernard was blamed for most of the pre-revolutionary trouble in the period of his governship and surely was confused time after time in deciding his problems. With the passage of the Stamp Act in 1765, however, he was clever enough to have the offensive packages of stamps landed at Castle Island. Of course the vigorous American opposition to the Stamp Act soon caused the law's repeal, with the return of all the stamps to England in the course of the following summer.

The poor refugees immortalized by Longfellow in his *Evangeline* arrived in Boston Harbor while Bernard was at the Castle. After a hasty consultation it was decided that the ships should leave the Harbor without landing. But hundreds of these poor folk had already been distributed around the Bay, and they stayed here for several years.

When Governor Bernard left Boston Harbor in 1769, a short period of calm was enjoyed, but it was only the lull before the storm. Lieutenant-Governor Hutchinson was now the commander of the Castle. The Castle was in need of repairs, and although the changes were of a superficial nature, the equivalent of fifty thousand dollars was expended to bring the fortress to its best possible condition. Colonel John Montrésor of His Majesty's Engineers in North America put the two hundred and ten guns at the island in fine condition, but we read that the Bostonians were reluctant to help him. Perhaps they felt that the guns might at some time in the near future be used against them, as did turn out to be the case.

On the second day of March, 1770, a dispute between a

soldier and a citizen started a feud which ended in blood-
shed three days later. On the night of March 5, the main
guard under Captain Preston was insulted and challenged,
a mob pelting them with sticks, snowballs, and stones. A
soldier who had been struck fired into the crowd; six of his
companions followed suit, and the world reads of the Boston Massacre. Three citizens had been killed outright and
two others died later. The 14th and 29th regiments were
forced to leave Boston as a result of this tragic event. The
enraged citizens had become so hostile that the men were
removed to the Castle to avoid further trouble. While at
the island, one of the soldiers composed the following
prophetic ditty:

> *Our fleet and our army will soon arrive*
> *Then to a bleak island you shall not us drive.*
> *In every house you shall have three or four*
> *And if that does not please you, you shall have*
> *half a score.*

The removal of British troops to Castle Island was of
course embarrassing to the English Parliament, whereas
assumption of full British control at Castle William was
equally offensive to the Province of Massachusetts. There
was no solution. On the tenth of September, 1770, Lieutenant-Governor Hutchinson withdrew the company of provincial soldiers and delivered the command of Castle Island
to Colonel Dalrymple. The 64th regiment of Colonel Leslie
from Halifax relieved Dalrymple, who sailed from Boston
with the troops on July 22, 1772.

When the Tea Act was passed in 1773, the Bostonians
resolved not to have the East India Company's tea at any
price. Hutchinson, now governor of Massachusetts, determined that the tea should be landed, so the ships were

docked at Griffin's Wharf. On December 16, 1773, a band of Bostonians dressed as Mohawk Indians boarded the ships and threw all the tea overboard into the Harbor.

Greatly humiliated, Parliament now closed Boston Harbor and sent General Gage to take charge of Massachusetts. When Gage fortified the town of Boston, he enraged the inhabitants of Massachusetts, and the fighting at Concord and Lexington soon prevented any further hope of reconciliation. As far as can be determined the regiment at the Castle did not participate in any of the early fighting. Colonel Leslie had started for Salem to seize powder and military stores, but had been forcibly detained at the ferries by the militia, so he returned to the Castle. He was later sent to destroy the American posts in Roxbury, but the best he could do was to burn five houses in Dorchester.

Although it is claimed that the Castle never participated in an actual engagement, it was under fire in the month of March, 1776. On the fifth of the month, Lord Percy planned to attack the Americans at Dorchester Heights, but a terrible gale came up which drove his transport ships far ashore at Governor's Island. In the Battle of Dorchester Heights the Castle batteries directed a withering fire against the various American emplacements on the mainland, but Continentals answered shot for shot. This engagement was the only serious battle in which the fort ever participated.

With the Americans firmly entrenched at Dorchester Heights, the British knew they would have to leave Boston, and Admiral Shuldam took charge of the departure. As they were passing down the Harbor, they stopped at Castle Island and started the task of destroying the fort. Dr. Warren tells us that they left the island ablaze on March 20, as they sailed for the outer Harbor. After many skirmishes on the other islands, the fleet left Boston, blowing up Boston Light as a final gesture.

We are fortunate in having the actual account of the destruction of Castle Island, as written down in the diary of Archibald Robertson, a young officer in the Royal Engineers. A few paragraphs from his important account follow:

"March 17, 1776.—Got to Castle William about 10 and in an hour saw the Rebels on the heights of Charles Town.

"[March] 18. In the Morning went to Castle William.

"19. Went to the Castle; found the mines all loaded but 12, which were again unloaded as the General wanted them not to be ready for some days.

"20th. Waited all the morning at Nantasket for want of a Boat. Got my Baggage taken out of the *Glen*. Between one and two found the Rebels had begun a new Work on Dorchester Point opposite Castle William. We fired at them from the Castle and by a Gun bursting had 7 men wounded. About two we observed about 21 Whale Boats set out from Dorchester Neck and row across to Thompson's Island, where they landed a small Cannon and pull'd it to the point and fired on our working Partys on Spectacle Island. At 3 o'clock Colonel Leslie came to the Castle from the General with orders to load the mines. We began immediately and had 63 done by 7 o'clock. As the night had the Appearance of Rain and the wind fair it was thought proper for the 64th to Embark, likewise to prevent any accident from the Rebels bringing a Gun and setting fire to any of the port fires, which might have been of bad Consequence. Accordingly at 8 o'clock 6 Companies Embarked and the Boats lay off untill the mines were fired. The Barracks and other houses were then set on fire and at 9 the Rear Guard consisting of 3 Companies, the Artillery, etc., Embarked and we got all safe on board the Transports. We got under way about 11 and went down near the Admiral in King Road."

Washington now sent a company of men across to the Castle to start refortifying the island. That ace of versatility, Paul Revere, spent some time in charge at the Castle and was successful in repairing most of the damage done. He replaced the broken and battered cascabels so that the pieces were soon fit for service. Castle Island, however, never again saw action.

Richard Gridley, the hero of Louisburg, supervised the erection of the new fortress in 1778 and added to the defense many guns taken from the wrecked British frigate *Somerset*. John Hancock assumed control of the Castle in 1779. The citizens of Boston helped to erect the battery, each working at least a day.

Hancock relinquished the title of commander at the fort in 1781 to Lieutenant-Governor Cushing. It was under Cushing that John Howard's famous prison reform system was tried in Massachusetts, with Castle Island as the location for this experiment. A small group of prisoners was sent from the mainland to what was to be the first state prison in Massachusetts. They were not the first prisoners at the Castle, however, for in the earlier days Indian prisoners had helped build the Castle, and King Philip had complained of it. Indian hostages confined at the Castle in 1721 had escaped from the island, causing an uproar in Boston before being caught. Edmund Andros had been able to get away for a brief time; but the man whose escapades became famous was Stephen Burroughs, a former Dartmouth College student. Burroughs participated in two escape attempts from the island, one of which was partially successful.

Governor Hancock kept control of the Castle until 1793,

when Lieutenant-Governor Samuel Adams assumed the
leadership. Adams became governor and held command of
the fort until 1797, when Governor Sumner became com-
mander-in-chief.

The United States and France were drifting apart, in
spite of the alliance of 1778, and war seemed reasonably
certain between these former friends. Due to this condition
Massachusetts decided to "sacrifice partial advantages to
general welfare," and offered the cession of the Castle to
the national government. Major Daniel Jackson arrived at
the Castle on the second of October 1798, and formally
accepted Castle William on behalf of the United States of
America.

In 1799 the execution of Joseph Perkins, ordered by the
President, attracted considerable attention. His crimes were
desertion and aiding the escape of prisoners. In the same
year the changing of the old name to Fort Independence
was carried out. President John Adams participated in the
ceremony held in August.

During the short war with France prisoners were landed
at Fort Independence, the first allotment of French sailors
arriving in July 1799. They did not cause as much trouble
as our own Massachusetts convicts. At one time 248 of
these unfortunate Frenchmen were imprisoned at Castle
Island. The last left our shores in March 1801.

The work of rebuilding Fort Independence was now
started, the first stone of the new structure being put into
place on May 7, 1801. Before many months had passed a
fine five-bastioned fortress was nearing completion. Lieutenant-Colonel Tousard was the constructing engineer.
When the fort was completed, Nehemiah Freeman, the
commander, named each of the five bastions. He called
the east bastion Winthrop; the southern bastion Shirley; the

north bastion Dearborn; the northwest bastion Adams, the western bastion Hancock.

Bostonians did not relinquish the century-old title of "Castle," and it is still known to the older residents and most sailors by that name. In 1805 Freeman remarked that the title "Fort Independence" would never be popular in Boston, and time has proved his statement.

Back in 1798 Congress had passed a bill taxing every sailor twenty cents a month to provide hospital accommodations ashore. Therefore, in 1799 a marine hospital, the first in New England, was started at Castle Island. Doctor Thomas Welsh contracted to treat the sick sailors at the building on Hospital Point.

Three incidents worthy of mention occurred in the next few years. On the twenty-third of November, 1805, John Fordice stabbed his wife in a quarrel, and she was thought to be dying. At the court martial Fordice claimed another man had alienated the affections of his wife. Fortunately, the lady recovered, and Fordice was let off with one hundred lashes. A year later, Benjamin Tarbell leaped into a well ninety feet deep to rescue a child who had fallen into the water. For this act of bravery, he was awarded ten dollars by the Massachusetts Humane Society. In the winter of 1809 two of the Castle soldiers started to walk across the ice from South Boston, but a blinding snowstorm came up and they fell through the ice. They were rescued by Messrs. White, More, and Gurney, who were also rewarded by the Society.

The British had planned to attack Boston as part of their campaign in the War of 1812. Learning of the formidable defense works on Castle Island, they changed their plans.

The Castle Island Records contain the list of officers subscribing to the Articles of War. Two signatures give us an

interesting case of brotherly love. Abel B. Chase, who signed
the list in June 1812, made quite a flourish under his name
which occupied the line below as well as that containing his
signature. In very small writing, inside of one of the flour-
ishes, is the following:

mon frere
Geo. E. Chase
1829

The Castle saw much activity during the second war with
England, but actual warfare was a thing of the past. The
distant booming of cannon during the fight between the
Chesapeake and the *Shannon* on June 1, 1813, was the nearest the soldiers came to active combat. A year later many
returned prisoners of war, including those captured from
the *Chesapeake*, came from Halifax. On the Fourth of July
1814, salutes were exchanged between Fort Independence
and Fort Warren, which was then located across the Harbor
on Governor's Island.

Castle Island has had its share of duels. At one time the
soldiers witnessed an encounter between Rand and Miller
on the shores of City Point. Fort Independence sent a boat
over to stop the affair, but Rand had already been killed.
Another duel occurred at Fort Independence on Christmas
Day many years ago. Possibly due to a quarrel at the Christmas Eve celebration, two of the officers in the Light Artillery fought a fatal duel at daybreak on December 25, 1817.
The duel ended with the death of Lieutenant Robert F.
Massie. His comrades decided that he should be buried on
the site of the counter. After the funeral they subscribed
for a handsome marble tombstone to be placed over his
grave, and for years the inscriptions on this monument drew
many visitors to Castle Island. Many good old South Boston

and Dorchester folk remember the gravestone on the glacis near the western battery, but it has been gone for years. The monument had the following inscription on the western panel:

> The officers of the U. S.
> Regiment of Lt. Art'y
> erected this monument
> as a testimony of their
> respect & friendship for
> an amiable man
> & Gallant officer.

The eastern panel contained the famous lines from Collin's ode:

> *Here honour comes, a Pilgrim gray,*
> *To deck the turf, that wraps his clay.*

On the northern side was the following:

> Beneath this stone are
> deposited the remains of
> Lieut. ROBERT F. MASSIE,
> of the
> U. S. Regt. of Light Artillery.

The fourth panel, formerly facing the south, read:

> Near this spot on the
> 25th, Decr, 1817, fell
> Lieut. Robert F. Massie,
> Aged 21 years.

The monument was moved from Fort Independence, along with Massie's skeleton, in 1892, and taken across the Harbor to Governor's Island. We may look in vain, however, for the monument on Governor's Island today. It was again moved with the skeleton, in 1908, and taken down to Deer

Island where it stood in the loneliest part of Resthaven Cemetery. In 1939 it was moved to Fort Devens in Ayer.

Every island has its unusual stories, but Castle Island has two that are quite remarkable. In 1818 a sea serpent came swimming past the two sentries stationed on the shore. The astonished men notified their superior, Colonel Harris, who verified the fact that it was this well known but never caught denizen of the deep. Exactly one hundred and fifty years before this strange occurrence, John Evered was drowned while fishing off the Castle. He had caught a "whale." In some manner the line became entangled about his waist, and he was pulled to his death beneath the waters of Boston Harbor. With whales and sea serpents cavorting in the waters near the Castle, the yachtsmen of the Harbor should perhaps be a trifle more circumspect in venturing out into Boston Bay.

On the twenty-sixth of May, 1827, a rather discouraged young man of eighteen enlisted in Battery H of the First Artillery. The records state that he had gray eyes and brown hair. The name he signed on the enrollment sheet was Edgar A. Perry. The boy was sent to Castle Island, where he served five months at Fort Independence. He was then transferred to Fort Moultrie, and Castle Island saw the last of Edgar Allan Poe, soon to surprise the country with his literary achievements. Without question Poe acquired at Fort Independence some of the atmosphere used in his writings. The "Cask of Amontillado" is based on the duel involving Robert Massie.

In 1834 Richard Henry Dana sailed as a common seaman from Boston. He waved goodby to Castle Island from the deck of the *Pilgrim* bound for California via Cape Horn. Two years later he returned from California, fresh from his struggles on the west coast. In *Two Years Before the Mast* he tells us of his return to Boston Harbor: "I took my place at the fore, and loosed and furled the royal five times between Rainsford Island and the Castle." Dana became a famous maritime lawyer in Boston.

On the twenty-third of May, 1808, Lieutenant Sylvanus Thayer, fresh from Dartmouth College, was sent over from Castle Island to erect water batteries on the shore of Governor's Island. After the completion of the shore defense, he was put in charge of building the enclosed redoubt at the top of the hill. This young lieutenant did work of such promise at Governor's Island that his superiors sent him to France to study under the great experts of that country. After many years away from home, he returned to take charge of the Military Academy at West Point. His achievements there can best be summarized by the inscription on his statue at the school—"Father of the Military Academy." Thayer left West Point in 1833, coming to Boston Harbor, where he began simultaneous operations at George's Island, Governor's Island, and Fort Independence.

Thayer was many years at his task. While he did good work at Castle Island, there was already so much of the Tousard fortress to be remodeled that he had little chance to show his own ability. However, Sylvanus Thayer is more responsible than any other man for the defenses of Boston Harbor. We should pay respect to perhaps the greatest fortification expert America has ever known. Army officers who have visited the best forts in the country admit that his masterpiece, Fort Warren, shows the best granite work in the United States. Thayer gave $300,000 for an academy at Braintree which now bears his name. He died in 1872 at the age of eighty-seven.

The great casemates at Fort Independence were each divided by board partitions into two sections. The first section of each casemate, the squad room, was used for barracks, and the other division comprised the gun chamber, and faced the glacis. The squad room looked in on the parade grounds.

The new commander was Brevet-Major George H. Thomas, who took over the Fort in 1851. A Mexican War veteran, he afterward distinguished himself in the Civil War. The second year of his service was one to be remembered by the sailors in the Harbor. Three fine ships were involved in serious accidents off the shores of the Castle. The first vessel to suffer was the schooner *Star*, which turned turtle and sank while on the way out of the Harbor. All hands were lost. A short time later the *Philadelphia* and the *Lizzie Williams* collided off the island, the latter craft sinking with the loss of several of her crew. Scores of accidents have taken place in this channel in the last hundred years.

Henry Lawrence Eustis was born at Castle Island in 1819. The son of General Abraham Eustis, he attended Harvard College, graduating with the class of 1838, which included such renowned men as James Russell Lowell and Charles Devens. Eustis followed the military traditions of the family by attending West Point, where he was a classmate of Ulysses S. Grant.

At the start of the Civil War, the three forts of the Harbor were found in unfavorable condition.

The Fourth Massachusetts Battalion was quartered for some time at the Castle, and among its honored members were Charles Francis Adams and William Francis Bartlett. In his *Autobiography*, Adams describes his life as a soldier at Castle Island. He did garrison duty at Fort Independence as a member of the Fourth, starting on April 24, 1861.

William Francis Bartlett enlisted on April 17, 1861. As a child he had roamed the shores of Winthrop with the great

Garibaldi, and later visited the famous soldier in Italy. He left the Junior Class at Harvard to train at Castle Island, staying at Fort Independence from May 25 until June 25. Bartlett was very happy during his month at the Castle, declaring it "the pleasantest and most fruitful that I remember." The year 1876 brought him to the end of his career. John Greenleaf Whittier honors this brave youth in verse:

> *As Galahad pure, as Merlin sage,*
> *What worthier knight was found*
> *To grace in Arthur's golden age*
> *The fabled table round?*

William Francis Bartlett did more to unite the two sections of our country after the Civil War than is commonly realized. In addition, he was the most conspicuous soldier New England sent to the Civil War, and his statue stands near the Hall of Flags entrance in the State House.

Major Stephenson, the commander of the Fourth Massachusetts, was to lose his life as a result of the War Between the States. As General Stephenson, he rode to his death in the Battle of the Wilderness.

In the year 1879, Fort Independence was given up as an active commissioned defense, in order that the garrisons might be concentrated at Fort Warren, and Ordnance-Sergeant Maguire was left in charge of the island. A few years before the fort was decommissioned, his son Joseph was born at the Castle.

Joseph Maguire began at a very early age to show ability as an oarsman. He had plenty of practice rowing back and forth from the Castle to school. He won the championship of the United States in 1894. This Castle Island prodigy repeated his national conquest in 1897, and in 1901 journeyed to Halifax to add to his list of triumphs.

After the army relinquished its claim to Fort Independence, the city of Boston made tentative plans to place the island in the hands of the Park Department. In 1891 a bridge was built from Marine Park to the Island, the Castle thus becoming identified with the mainland and South Boston.

All Boston celebrated June 29, 1896, as Farragut Day. Thousands crowded the streets of South Boston, and hundreds of children walked out on the pier to Castle Island. Many of the boys and girls wore Farragut Day buttons, which read: "South Boston Historical Society, Farragut Day, June 29, '96." This badge entitled the children to a free ride on two little boats, the *Ella* and the *Pearl*.

At two-thirty the *Ella* left City Point Landing for the Island, loaded with children. As it neared the Castle, the boys and girls at the landing started a rush for the float, and Officer Pickham was swept aside. The children ran down to the raft and crowded the runway. Suddenly the float turned turtle. The dead were all boys: Lawrence McDowell, twelve; James F. Cole, eleven; James S. Washburn, nine; John A. O'Leary, eleven. Two young girls were trampled upon and required hospital treatment. The accident was due to the poor construction of the float, and to the lack of adequate protection at the landing.

When the Spanish War broke out in 1898, the United States took the fort away from the city, and made it into a mine and torpedo station.

On July 22, 1898, five hundred engineers and friends gathered at Castle Island and watched two of the mines blown up. The mines were anchored one thousand feet from the easterly side of the island and were marked with red flags. The cable had been connected with the switch ashore, and all was in readiness. While thousands cheered from the City Point Pier, Sergeant Hart moved the switch, and a two-hundred-foot column of water shot into the air. A moment passed before the sound of the explosion reached the island.

On December 6 of that year, the engineers were moving the mines to the southeastern side of the island. Suddenly, without warning, a great explosion rocked the city. When the smoke and dust had cleared there was a gaping hole in the seawall. A minute or two before three men had been unloading a wagon on the spot. They were Engineer Hiram Vaughn; Peter Brennan, the driver of the wagon; and a civilian, James Ryan. Not only were these three men blown to pieces, but Ordnance-Sergeant Maurice McGrath, three hundred feet away, was killed. Sergeant Hart, who had been standing behind the powder magazine, escaped injury.

With the Spanish War over, the island was turned back to the city, and once more the residents of Boston enjoyed their precious view from the ramparts of Fort Independence. It has been conservatively estimated that as many as seventy thousand people have visited this grand old fortress on a Sunday afternoon.

Bostonians were again disturbed in 1902, when the United States Government announced its decision to take over Castle Island for the Lighthouse Department. The trouble began when the War Department decided to take over Lovell's Island, which borders the outer Harbor. The Lighthouse Department had been occupying John Lovell's old island continuously since 1874 and were now looking for a new home. Fortunately, after strong controversy, the Lighthouse Department was forced to make other plans.

In the summer of 1907 the War Department asked for bids on a few guns that had been lying about on the glacis of the fort ever since the Civil War. A local junk dealer purchased these veterans of a former day, and taking the fourteen-thousand-pound monsters off into deep water, used dynamite to break the guns into smaller pieces.

The United States Government, in spite of two previous failures, tried in 1909 to make an immigration station of the Castle. The renewed efforts ended in defeat.

The Government at Washington again wanted the entire island for the Lighthouse Department in 1911. Strenuous objections from Mayor Fitzgerald and Senator Henry Cabot Lodge induced Senator Frye to change the location. The same year saw the summer school started at the island. The sick children from four schools in South Boston marched two by two over the long planked bridge leading to Castle Island, and attended classes inside the fort. The school was continued for several years. On March 27, 1918, the Boston Fire Department made a record trip across the bridge to put out a fire raging in the casemates.

For many years the inhabitants of Boston have argued over the chain which did or did not stretch across the Harbor for wartime protection. I would like to settle the "ghost" of the chain for all time. Caleb Snow, Nathaniel Shurtleff, and Jerome V. C. Smith did not mention the chain in their respective surveys of Boston Harbor, and James Stark and Melvin Sweetser are also silent about this connection between Governor's and Castle Islands. John Winthrop, John Josselyn, and Samuel Sewall have made no reference to it. *The Boston Post* printed in a Sunday edition in 1933 a sketch of the chain stretching between the two islands, and a small pamphlet on the islands in 1932 mentions the chain, stating that the winch was still to be seen at Governor's Island. This is wrong.

I have been at Governor's Island over two hundred times, and I have interviewed a well-known resident of Winthrop who thirty years ago lived on the island for five years.

Neither of us has seen anything resembling this winch. There never was a chain going from Governor's to Castle Island. It is not reasonable to assume that all the great Harbor authorities have forgotten to mention a chain if it had existed. The only evidence we have that such a chain existed has been written within the last thirty-five years, and in no case is a source mentioned.

In my correspondence with the War Department it has been definitely settled that no chain has existed. A sentence from a letter of September 8, 1934, should suffice:

"An examination of such records thought likely to afford the desired information has resulted in failure to find any record of the chain having been stretched across Boston Harbor."

There are two probable sources for the various rumors which are now in existence. The first is in the Boston Town Records of 1741. The town was worried in that year about adequate fortifications to protect Boston, and in March 1741 a committee visited the area between Governor's and Castle Islands, made a survey of the situation, and reported back to the selectmen that a series of piers could be placed across the Harbor for an estimated cost of £18,200. The selectmen decided to petition the General Court for the consideration of this scheme. Quoting from the Massachusetts Archives, we learn that "from the middle century box in the lower battery of the Castle N.E. by N. to Governor's Island point is 1457 feet. Now, ... build 22 pears, 30 ft. square of timber and fill with stone, sink them cornerwise, eleven on each side of the channel, and leave twelve feet between each pier. . . . . . Thus 203 feet is open in the middle to traffic, and in case of necessity, two hulks could be sunk in the space, blocking the channel." The General Court referred the scheme to a committee, but nothing was done about it. The sketch presented with the petition is copied herewith.

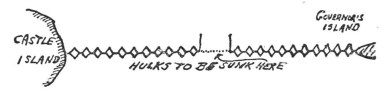

The same idea, with variations, was proposed down through the years, but nothing was ever done. In the Civil War a suggestion was made that the channel be guarded with a chain, but in the *Life of John A. Andrew* we read that this remained merely a suggestion. Thus we see that, judging from original records, no chain ever stretched across the Harbor.

According to an old legend, there is a curse on all who dare to visit Castle Island. Some time before the Revolution, as the story goes, an English gentleman lived on the island with his charming young daughter. She was in love with a young American boy. Her father, however, had other plans and determined that she should marry a British officer, also in love with the girl. The two suitors agreed to fight a duel for the young lady, and the American was killed. The girl, determined to join her lover, committed suicide. The British officer, heartbroken, rushed down to the dock and plunged into the channel, crying as he went that he would put a curse on all who ever came near the island. Some sailors still believe that the many shipwrecks near the Castle are to be blamed on this curse. There have been many other suicides on the island in the last few decades. In 1903 a man jumped from the wharf into the ocean, and his body was never recovered. Years ago a Somerville man was found in one of the casemates with a bullet in his head. Regardless of the story's romantic appeal, there is very little historical foundation to the tale. It may have been spun by the old minstrel Rochford.

Talking with an elderly man at the island some time ago, I learned of a gruesome discovery in an abandoned casemate which had been sealed up. In 1905 workmen were repairing the interior of the fort, and opened up a section of the wall that had been closed for many years. They were horrified to find a skeleton dressed in an old military costume. After some time spent in efforts to learn the man's identity, they gave up in despair and buried his remains in the graveyard.

Over the causeway built in 1927 we can now motor out to the island from the city in ten minutes, and by visiting the parade grounds of the old fortress pass into a different world. The parapets invite the visitor. The port of the Puritans stands before us. While still on the ramparts, we make a short survey of the island. The island's shape suggests the head of some prehistoric monster, the causeway serving as the neck.

In the spring of 1933 a commanding monument fifty-two feet high was erected in front of the fortress to commemorate the life of Donald McKay, the famous East Boston shipbuilder. Standing proudly on the esplanade, this graceful shaft built of Maine granite greets the various ships coming up the Harbor. The profile of McKay is set in relief on the northeastern panel, and as the inscription states, his genius "produced ships of a beauty and speed before unknown which swept the seven seas." These graceful ships will never be replaced in the memory of the true sailors of America by the modern steel giants. The expense of the monument to Donald McKay was borne privately, President Franklin D. Roosevelt being among those who sub-scribed to the memorial.

During World War II the island was used for one of the harbor command posts, and a substantial building was erected on top of old Dearborn Bastion. From this post the entire harbor defenses were under control, with the various submarine nets and mining stations always ready for any eventuality. After the war the building was torn down, and Castle Island's five-starred fortification reverted to its usual state.

At the height of a gale on the morning of March 10, 1964, a Slick Airways cargo liner undershot a landing at Logan Airport, Boston, and crashed at Castle Island Docks. All three men aboard were killed.

Fort Independence's genial host, Dan Sullivan, runs the canteen on Castle Island. He told me of the construction of the community fishing pier a few years ago, dedicated to Fire Lieutenant John J. McCorkle, who, with four of his associates, perished in the Trumbull Street Fire of October, 1, 1964. The MDC has taken over the island, and plans to open the parade grounds soon to the public.

So we leave the venerable island, trusting that for count-less generations it will be cherished by the people of Boston. Castle Island should remain a treasured possession of all New Englanders.

4

NIX'S MATE AND BIRD ISLANDS

There are two islands down the Harbor which have long stood for tragedy and terror in the history of Boston Bay. More than fifteen notorious pirates have been buried on Bird Island and Nix's Mate, and many an honest sailor has been startled by the skeleton of a buccaneer hanging in chains on one of these islands. Due to the inroads of man and nature, both islands have practically vanished from the Harbor. While a small part of the original Nix's Mate Island still remains, Bird Island has been absorbed by the airport.

Governor Winthrop tells an exciting story of several men who were frozen in at Bird Island in 1634. When they were coming up the Harbor from Deer Island, the passage became so difficult that they were forced to stop at Bird Island for the night. The group must have suffered terribly on the island; it was so cold that the Harbor froze over before morning and they were able to walk over to the mainland with the coming of dawn.

In the Town Records for 1650 we read that "Tho⁵ Munt

hath liberty to mow the marsh at Bird Island this yeare."
We cannot tell how many years Munt gathered hay from
this island, but we do know that in 1658, "Bird Island is lett
to James Euerill & Rich Woody for sixty yeares, paying
12 d siluer or a bushel of salt every first of March to y^e
town Treasurer."

The early history of Nix's Mate Island is more obscure
than that of Bird Island. We have many different stories as
to why the island is so named. The legend which is often
told down the Harbor concerns the mate of a Captain Nix.
The mate was accused of murdering his captain and was
taken to the island to be hanged for the crime. Before he
was swung off into eternity, he is alleged to have declared
that as proof of his innocence the island would some day
disappear. Although this mythical allegation has, to a certain
extent, been literally confirmed by the diminished island,
there are two indisputable factors which prevent our accep-
tance of the legend. The first is that none of the pirates
brought to this island was still alive when landed on the
shore; the second is that at the time the island was first
called Nix in 1636, no man had been executed for a marine
murder in the Massachusetts Colony.

Many students of history have made conjectures as to the
real reason for the island's name. Alexander Corbett believed that what we now know as Gallop's Island was once
owned by a man named Nix, and the smaller island, also
owned by Nix, was known as Nix's Mate. Moses Sweetser
published in his *Handbook* an alleged letter written by a
"Rich: Burbeck," the source of which he does not give. I
will quote part of it.

"And so when Master Codington saide, What do you
Dutch call that, Dirke said, 'Nixie Schmalt,' I do not know
how to spell it, but it meaneth the Wail of the Water Spirit,

or the Water Spirit is chiding. But Master Codington thought it was the name of the Iland, and set it down on the map he had Nix his Mate Island."

The first historical record about Nix's Mate dates back to 1636, when John Gallop was granted the twelve acres on "Nixes Iland, to enjoy to him & his heirs forever, if the iland bee so much." So we see that even in 1636 the island was evidently washing away.

Nix's Mate passed out of the possession of the Gallop family after the death of John Gallop in 1650, and later Edward Tyng became the owner. He sold part of the island to Joseph Rock on August 16, 1669. While Rock owned Nix's Mate, one of the early tragedies of the Harbor took place just off the shore. Josiah Hunting, Ebenazar Blackman, and several other gentlemen went down the Harbor to fish, and when they were off the northern shore, a squall of wind came up, tipping over the boat and throwing the occupants into the water. Blackman, who could not swim, grabbed at Hunting while they were struggling in the water, but, according to Hunting, "slipped his hold and I saw said Blackman no more." Joseph Rock deeded three fourths of the Island to Edward Bromfield for six pounds in the year 1683.

The first pirate to be discussed in our survey is Thomas Pound, Boston Harbor cartographer and pirate unique. Although at one time in his career he was under sentence to be hanged for piracy, Pound lived to die a natural death in England. His fine chart of Boston Harbor was drawn about 1685, and it was such a masterpiece that it was used as a guide by the leading cartographers of the world for the next sixty years.

After Nelson led the attack against Sir Edmund Andros at Fort Hill, Pound evidently decided to cast his lot with the unfortunate baronet, and his plans led him to Bull's Tavern on the eighth of August, 1689, to form a plot which would help his former leader. Although the actual plans will probably never be known, it is safe to assume that Pound and his companions schemed to capture ships and supplies outside Boston Harbor. By these acts of piracy they would thus challenge the *Rose*, the government vessel, to come out and fight the pirate ship. The *Rose*, manned by Andros sympathizers, was to accompany Pound's ship to Rhode Island, where Andros would be waiting for them to sail to France in an effort to aid their deposed King.

With this plan in mind, Pound and six companions left the tavern about midnight and boarded a schooner tied up at the wharf. Slipping quietly down the Harbor, they were soon abeam of Long Island where the ship dropped anchor. They satisfied the owner, Thomas Hawkins, by saying that they had changed their plans and were going fishing instead of to Nantasket, their stated destination. Just before daylight they weighed anchor, and on passing Lovell's Island, heard a boat being pushed off the beach. Soon five armed men boarded the schooner. Pound now announced that he was in command, and owner Hawkins gave in. The schooner sailed in an easterly direction until about thirty miles off the Brewsters, where the pirates stopped a sloop and purchased eight pennyworth of fish. Skirting the shore line until near Halfway Rock off Portland, they captured a fishing ketch, and after changing boats with the fishermen continued on their way. Falmouth, Maine, was reached the following Monday, and the pirates communicated with some of the soldiers at Fort Loyal. The pirates were successful in winning over seven of the enlisted men, who fled from the fort that night with most of the powder and guns in the stronghold. Pound and his men were responsible for the subsequent surrender of the defenseless little fort during a battle with Indians.

Thomas Pound now continued his piratical career by capturing the sloop *Brother's Adventure*, getting some badly needed provisions from her. On September 30 there sailed from Boston Harbor the sloop *Mary*, armed and prepared to clear New England waters of Thomas Pound and his crew. The *Mary* caught up with the pirates at Tarpaulin Cove, and after a short but bloody encounter, her crew boarded the pirate craft and captured the fourteen remaining pirates. Pound, seriously wounded, was taken to Boston with the others of the crew. As far as his piratical days were concerned, his career was over.

Shurtleff and Sweetser, usually very reliable in their facts, made the mistake of writing that both Hawkins and Pound were executed. This is not the case. After the trial, the two men sailed on the refitted *Rose*, which was attacked by a French privateer. Hawkins was killed in the battle, as was Captain John George. On reaching England, Pound was appointed Captain of the frigate *Sally Rose* and in 1699 retired to Middlesex County in England. He died in 1703.

Captain John Quelch is the next subject for discussion, and special attention should be paid to one of the members of his crew, John Lambert. The remains of John Lambert still repose in King's Chapel Burying Grounds. In August 1703, Quelch sailed in command of the brigantine *Charles* from Marblehead. The pirates locked the real captain in his room before the ship had left the harbor and, after reaching the high seas, threw him overboard. In the next few months Quelch captured nine Portuguese ships, with each pirate in the crew making a small fortune. Returning home the middle of the following May, the *Charles* dropped anchor at Marblehead and the men went ashore, apparently believing that they would not be molested. When the authorities in Boston heard of the ship's arrival, however, they sent Attorney-General Paul Dudley to capture the crew of the pirate ship. He brought Quelch, Lambert, and five other pirates back to Boston with him.

There were many buccaneers still at large, however, and late one night Samuel Sewall was notified that there were "9 or 11 Pirats, double arm'd, seen in a Lone-house" at Cape Ann. He arose immediately and alarmed the soldiers of the countryside. There was great excitement along the North Shore until the capture of these notorious men was effected. The twenty-fifth of June saw twenty-five of these pirates safely imprisoned at the Boston jail. Only seven were eventually sentenced to death, as the rest were given pardons upon the condition that they should enter the Queen's service.

June 20, 1704, the Silver Oar, the emblem of the Court of Admiralty, was carried in front of the condemned pirates as they made their way down to Scarlett's Wharf, located at the foot of Fleet Street. They were taken to the gallows erected out over the water. Cotton Mather, the well-known Boston clergyman, went in a boat to give the men their final admonitions. The surrounding shore was lined with men and women, and Broughton's Hill, overlooking the gallows, was crowded. The spectators eagerly waited to hear the last words of notorious Captain Quelch. He informed the gathering that he was on the verge of eternity merely because he had brought money into New England, money that could not be said to be dishonest. He told his listeners to be careful lest they also be hanged. "I am condemned only upon circumstances," he concluded.

When the scaffold dropped from under the seven men,

there was such a screech from the women present it was heard by the wife of Samuel Sewall at her house, located a mile from the scene of the execution. This was in spite of a strong wind blowing from the opposite direction.

The bodies of all the pirates but one were taken down the Harbor and either buried or hung in chains on one of the two islands used for this ghastly purpose. Sewall gave permission for the body of John Lambert, a member of a prominent Salem family, to be smuggled up to what is now King's Chapel Burying Grounds and interred in the family lot at midnight. Although the pirate was not given a tombstone, the graves of his wife and his son in the same lot are still to be seen. Thus we have a blood-thirsty pirate buried in the peaceful haven of Boston's own King's Chapel Graveyard.

In 1724 two pirates, John Rose Archer and William White, were executed in Boston and later taken to Bird Island. The head of their master, Captain John Phillips, had been brought into Boston in a pickle barrel. John Rose Archer, after his execution, was hung in chains at Bird Island, with the body of William White buried in the sand underneath the gibbet. Before the execution both men were penitent, and spoke against the evils of drink. White declared that he "was drunk when enticed aboard the Pyrate." John Rose Archer made this impressive remark on the gallows: "I could wish that masters of Vessels would not use their men with so much severity, as many of them do, which exposes us to great Temptations." That noted diarist of Boston, Jeremiah Bumstead, took a large party of friends and relatives down to Bird Island a week after the execution to see the body of Archer swinging in chains at the lonely spot.

Another pirate, William Fly, was strung up in chains at

Nix's Mate. We quote from John Campbell's *News-Letter* of July 14, 1726:

"On Tuesday the 12th Instant, about 3 p.m. were executed here for Piracy, Murder, & c. Three of the Condemned Persons mentioned in our last, viz. *William Fly*, *Capt. Samuel Cole*, Quartermaster, and *Henry Greevill*, the other viz. *George Condick*, was Repriev'd at the Place of Execution. . . . Fly behaved himself very unbecomingly even to the last; however advised Masters of Vesels not to be Severe and Barbarous to their Men, which might be a reason why so many turned Pirates. . . . Their Bodies were carried in a Boat to a Small Island called Nick's Mate, about 2 Leagues from the Town, where the abovesaid Fly was hung up in Irons, as a Spectacle for the Warning of others, especially Sea faring Men; the other Two were buried there."

Far more than two hundred years have elapsed since the last pirate was buried in the shifting sands of Nix's Mate and Bird Island. The sinister part of their careers now over forever, the two islands were assigned more pastoral duties. Nix's Mate was advertised from time to time for grazing purposes, and in 1735 the New England *Courant* carried an advertisement of sixteen lines stressing its suitability along this line.

William Price, who copied many of John Bonner's masterpieces, made a view of the southeastern part of Boston in 1745, dedicating the print to Peter Faneuil. In the lower left-hand corner of the print Bird Island is identified and on Bird Island, Price has put a "Fort George." The inscription plainly reads "Fort George on Bird Island," but history is strangely silent about this fort. Perhaps Price was confused at the time, but possibly some day we may find evidence to verify his drawing of more than two centuries ago.

A rather amusing incident took place on September 18, 1863, when "four gentlemen ran their boat onto Nix's Mate and found themselves in the water." They were rescued by parties from Snow's Island, or Gallop's Island, as it is known today, and according to the newspaper account, returned to their homes much wiser gentlemen.

So the next time you sail by the low marker at Bird Island or the high cement pyramid at Nix's Mate, think back two hundred years to the days of Quelch, Archer, and Fly, whose skeletons were buried in the shifting sand bars around the two islands.

5

THOMPSON'S ISLAND

After a short journey across the deep waters of Dorchester Bay, we approach the landing at Thompson's Island. The Farm and Trades School occupies the entire 157 acres of David Thompson's old home, and the well-trained boys of the organization help us moor our boat at the float. We jump down on the landing raft, walk along the pier, and reach the island itself. It is a beautiful spot, with gardens, shrubbery, and hundreds of fine trees offering a pleasing background to the splendid buildings of the school. As we stand before the site of the administration building, let us think back three centuries to the day in September 1621 when Myles Standish landed here on a trip from Plymouth.

Captain Standish had left the Pilgrim settlement in an open sailboat to explore the coast line of Massachusetts Bay, as well as to make trading arrangements with the Indians of this region. His party of thirteen had expected to reach Boston Harbor the same day they left Plymouth, but it was not until the following night that they anchored off Thompson's Island. Standish and the others, including William Trevore, went ashore the next morning. Back in London, David Thompson had asked Trevore to pick out a likely island that Thompson could use for a trading post, so Trevore took possession of the island for his London friend.

Myles Standish believed, and Shurteleff contended, that the Indians never made their home at this island, but a well-stocked museum at the school proves that they were mistaken. Mortars, pestles, axes, plummets, spearheads, and arrowheads that were dug on the Island are in the collection, and all point to long-established homes of the red men at Thompson's Island. The Indian residents were probably all killed in the pestilence that swept the Massachusetts area a few years before the white man arrived. Morton of Merrymount speaks of this terrible plague.

Thus we see that Standish explored and Trevore claimed Thompson's Island nine years before the Puritans arrived in Boston Bay. There were six distinct settlements in the same area by 1626: Wessagussett, Mount Wollaston, Mishawum, Shawmut, Winnisimmet, and Hull. They had possibly fifty people at this time.

Shortly after Gorges' colony of 1622 had settled at Wessagussett, another party landed at Little Harbor, New Hampshire, on the west side of the Piscataqua River. Among them was David Thompson for whom Trevore had claimed Thompson's Island. Thompson is mentioned in the Council of New England Records, being linked with another early settler whose name is perpetuated by a Boston Harbor island: "Mr. Thompson is ordered to pay unto Leo. Peddock £10 towards his paynes for his last Imployments to New England." While working for the Council in London, Thompson had naturally become quite interested in America, and his name disappears from the records after December 3, 1622, when he "propounded" for the transportation

of ten persons to New England. As Thompson was not
wealthy enough to assume the responsibility for all the
expenses of the undertaking, he mortgaged one fourth of his
new lands to three other men. The Massachusetts Historical
Society published the indenture in 1875. I quote from the
records:

"Imprimus, whereas the Councell haue granted vnto
thaboue named David Thompson . . . one Iland & being in &
vpon the coaste of New England. . . . At the end of five
years the iland is to be divided into 4 parts whereof Thompson is to have three and others one."

Thompson's settlement became firmly established on the
Piscataqua River, near the mouth of the westerly branch.
The ruins of the first house in what is now New Hampshire
are on the peninsula there, and were described by Samuel
Maverick when he visited the location in 1660. David
Thompson, in spite of his pleasant situation on the Piscataqua, was anxious to come down to his island, and, after
spending three years at what is now known as Odiorne's
Point, moved to Boston Harbor in 1626. Thompson built a
substantial home near the eastern shore, just south of the
center of the island bearing his name. Part of this building
was discovered in 1889 by students digging on the bank.
The old cellar floor was almost intact, but the eastern and
southern walls had fallen over the cliff years before. Bowls
and stems of long Dutch pipes were unearthed in the ruins.
This building was probably the first house in Boston Harbor, for we can find no evidence of the erection of any earlier edifice. Thompson died before 1630, as the tax paid by
the Thompson family for their share in the eviction of
Morton of Merrymount was charged to Mrs. Thompson,
which would not have been the case had her husband been
alive.

Thompson's wife, at different times called Amias, Ems, and Aimes, was the daughter of William Cole of Plymouth, England. She married Samuel Maverick of Noddle's Island some time before 1632. For a while they lived in a house located where the Marine Hospital now stands in Chelsea, then moved to Noddle's Island. In 1635 she wrote to Robert Trelawny from "Nottell's Island." As soon as she and her son John had left Thompson's Island, the Massachusetts Bay Colony took possession. In 1634 the Court granted the island to Dorchester.

John Thompson, the first white child born in what is now New Hampshire, was then a boy of nine living with his mother and step-father at Noddle's Island. For fourteen years Dorchester collected taxes from residents on Thompson's Island, and in 1639 the yearly tax was set at twenty pounds. According to Orcutt, the Dorchester historian, this money helped pay for the first free public school in America supported by a direct tax on the people. He claims that the first schools in other towns, Boston included, were either private or were not supported by public taxes. Thomas Waterhouse was the first schoolmaster of Dorchester.

John Thompson bought a house in Charlestown in 1648, giving as security Thompson's Island. But Thompson soon lost control of his property. In 1650 he was in debt to two Bristol merchants to the sum of £163. The note he gave was never taken up, so the island passed out of the Thompson family forever.

Some time later, Simon Lynde, a wealthy and popular resident of Tremont Hill owned the island outright and presented it to his young son Benjamin, confirming the gift in his will. Benjamin Lynde grew up to be one of the best-educated lawyers in America, and was a classical scholar of note. Let us read from his poem on Thompson's Island, probably written in imitation of *Echoes from the Sabine Farm* by Horace, the Roman poet who lived just before the birth of Christ:

> *To save these queries about our isle,*
> *Kind heaven which placed it well does on it smile;*
> *In form triangular, its gradual sides*
> *Rise from the arms of Neptune's gentle tides.*
> *Southwest of Royal William's Citadel*
> *On Castle Isle, by Romer finsh'd well*
> *Heart of the Province, and its piercing eye,*
> *With bulwarks strong, and bright artillery,*
> *Guarding all parts that near adjacent lye.*
> *Two rural neighbor towns ly west of it,*
> *Close, on the south, a Cliff lifts up its brow,*
> *High, prominent o'er the parting stream below;*
> *From whence the Native's fate-predicting squaw*
> *Their ruin, and the Briton's Rise foresaw;*
> *That Heaven's swift plagues shall quickly sweep away*
> *The Indians 'round the Massachusetts Bay.*
> *But she (while they her rage prophetic mock)*
> *Flings headlong down from the steep craggy rock;*
> *Mu-Squantum! from her dying murmers fell,*
> *And thence call'd Squantum Neck, (as ancients tell).*
> *A narrow gut, deep, swift, and curling tide,*
> *This spacious neck from Thompson's Isle divide.*
> *Thus having given of Thompson's Isle the site,*
> *Which to review is anybody's right*
> *"Of special love," said he (my father) "this gift receive,*
> *And here at pleasure may you happy live."*
> *With grateful heart his Blessing I received*
> *For here with joy and dutiful regard*
> *In all my rural comforts he had shared.*

The trying days of the American Revolution were now at hand. After the British established themselves in Boston,

American troops landed on Thompson's Island and burned all the buildings, orchards, and crops, the blaze lighting up the entire section as darkness fell. When the British were finally forced to leave the Harbor in March 1776, they were cannonaded by Colonel Tupper from the East Head at Thompson's Island.

Benjamin Lynde's daughter married the Rev. William Walter, who was a Loyalist, and his petition to the English Government can still be seen in the public Record Office in London. He sold their share in the island for £2000 to George Minot.

We shall now consider the original organization of the Farm and Trades School.

The Boston Asylum for Indigent Boys had been incorporated in 1814, with William Phillips and James Lloyd among those whose names appear in the act of incorporation. The trustees bought as a home Sir William Phips' former residence, located on the corner of Salem and Charter Streets. In 1832 John D. Williams headed an organization which became "The Boston Farm School Society." After purchasing Thompson's Island, the group sent the Reverend E. M. P. Wells down the Harbor to begin construction work. He started operations on Easter Monday, April 8, 1833, and the boys who accompanied him began farming the same morning. Wells, a veteran of the War of 1812, continued working at the island for the next six months. He was the first to make a distinction between the worthy and the delinquent boys. The Wells Memorial for Workingmen is a splendid commemorative organization in Boston honoring this far-seeing minister whom Phillips Brooks called a "remarkable man."

Captain Daniel Chandler, active in the War of 1812, assumed office on October 26, 1833, as the second superintendent of the school. In 1834 the state transferred the island from Norfolk County to Suffolk County, and it was now under the jurisdiction of Boston. In 1835 an act of the Massachusetts Legislature united the Boston Asylum for Indigent Boys with the Farm School. Chandler left the island in 1839 to become superintendent of the House of Industry in South Boston, a position he filled until his death in 1847.

When Chandler left the island, a period of crisis was at hand for the school. The great panic of 1837 had left its mark on Thompson's Island; building construction was at a standstill. Edwin J. Mills was in charge for three months, Payson Williams stayed on twice that length of time, and James Locke served over a year before being asked to resign.

The members of the Board of Directors were now desperate and realized that a strong man was needed to put the school on a sound footing. At this time the Board asked Cornelius Conway Felton, a professor at Harvard College, to become superintendent. Allowed to retain his professorship at the college, Felton would lend the needed dignity to the school on Thompson's Island. Cornelius Felton accepted the offer, and from that time much progress was made. His influence lasted for years, and he took an interest in the school even after he was elected president of Harvard College in 1860.

Theodore Lyman was made president of the Board of Directors in 1841. His first act was to obtain Robert Morrison as superintendent, and during his term of office the main buildings were completed, and the enrollment, which had dropped off to forty-one, soon became normal. President Lyman, who had always been an admirer of the efforts of Eleazer Wells to distinguish between worthy and delinquent boys, asked the Massachusetts Legislature to take steps for their segregation. As a result of Lyman's hard work, the first state school for boys in the world was opened at Westboro, Massachusetts.

Gradually, the islanders became accustomed to the marine aspect of their location. In 1842 the boys made their first cruise to Boston, thus inaugurating a custom that lasted for half a century. When their boat reached Boston, the boys formed in line and marched up to City Hall, where they listened to an address by the mayor. After visiting many of the historical points in the city, they assembled on Boston Common, where the afternoon was spent with their relatives and friends. As the sun began to set, they started for the steamboat landing and finally crossed the bay on the school boats, the *Vision*, the *Annie*, and the *Polka*.

On April 29 of the same year, a large party of boys accompanied by their instructor was returning from the outer Harbor in the *Polka* when the boat capsized and twenty-five of the passengers lost their lives. It was the worst tragedy in the history of the school. Only the day before, relatives and directors had visited the island and had given twenty-seven boys permission to go on a fishing trip down the Harbor as a reward for their fine work. Mr. Oakes, an experienced sailor, and Mr. Peabody, a teacher, had charge of the trip, which the boys greatly enjoyed. At the close of the day the party was returning to the school against a headwind, passing so close to the eastern head of the island that they were given a cheer by their schoolmates who did not make the trip. Having stood for Spectacle Island, the boat was in the act of tacking for the purpose of making the landing dock when suddenly over she went, sinking instantly. The wooden box that held bait floated free, and four of the boys clung to it, but the other twenty-three and the two men were drowned. The four boys were brought into Boston by boats that had rushed to the scene. This tragedy left only half of the students to continue at school and to work on the farm.

When Nathaniel Hawthorne was active on the Boston waterfront, he visited Thompson's Island many times, and on one of his visits he took an extensive walk around the island, examining with interest the products of the farm. He saw the "wheat in sheaves on the stubble-field; oats somewhat blighted and spoiled; great pumpkins elsewhere; pastures; mowing grounds—all cultivated by the boys." Hawthorne comments on the residence, a "great brick building, painted green, and standing on the summit of a rising ground, exposed to the winds of the bay."

Another visitor in 1845, greatly impressed by the island, was reminded of the story of Latona, who had an island created in the sea as a refuge for her children. He also tells of the excitement at the island when the relatives and friends visit the boys.

This writer, John R. Dix, noticed one little boy who had no caller. The child sat in the reception room, his blue eyes filled with tears as he realized that there was no one to greet him.

"Poor little fellow, how I pitied him! I declare that I never longed for molasses candy, or something of that kind before: and I made a mental resolution that in the future I would never visit such places without a provision for a similar contingency. . . ."

Leaving the island in the winter has always been a difficult problem, but in 1856 the boys were able to walk over the ice, and one of the managers of the school rode in a sleigh from City Point right up to the door of the main building!

The same year, Morrison left Thompson's Island, returning to his home in Portsmouth, New Hampshire. The next three years he was mayor of Portsmouth, and his picture hangs in the city hall there. His place at Thompson's Island was taken by William A. Morse, who had come there in 1850 as supervisor of the farm.

Morse remained at the island during the trying days of the Civil War, when over 150 undergraduates, graduates, and teachers of the school on Thompson's Island enlisted. He was active in over twelve different positions in this period, including the following: purchasing agent, accountant, secretary, headmaster, nurse, captain of the boat, head of the graduate employment agency, blacksmith, agricultural expert, head slaughterer, minister, and organist! Under his leadership the new barn was erected, the first steamer was purchased, the first boys' band in America was organized, and printing was introduced.

While Morse was superintendent of the Farm and Trades School, Nathaniel Bradstreet Shurtleff made a trip to the island. The future mayor of Boston gives the following description of the Thompson's Island of 1870:

"On the southwest side [of the island] is a salt water pond of several acres, into which once flowed a creek that in ancient times was dignified by the name of river. Thompson's Island Bar, which projects toward Squantum, has long been a noted locality for its delicious clams. The form of the island as shown on the charts is very much like that of a young unfledged chicken, looking toward the east. Deep water lies to the north and west, shoal water to the east and south."

After a long and happy period of office at the Farm School, William Appleton Morse resigned as superintendent in 1888 and was succeeded by Charles Henry Bradley, author of an unpublished history of the school. It was in

Bradley's first year that the "Cottage Row" plan of government and recreation was started in rather an unusual way.
While baseball, swimming, and football came and went, the
one interest which never flagged was that of Cottage Row,
the miniature city the boys built, cared for, and governed.

In the summer of 1888 the boys were given some cast-off
bedticking. This they made over into tents, which they soon
arranged in rows at the northern end of the playground.
When the autumn weather arrived, some of the boys rein-
forced their tents with boards, but the cold winter soon
forced them inside. With the coming of spring, some of the
boys believed that a wooden cottage could be built to take
the place of the tents. With the help of Superintendent
Bradley, they planned and erected a small cottage, the
manual training department being utilized in this rather
novel venture.

Cottage after cottage was built, until in 1891 Superintendent Bradley decided to limit the number of buildings to
twelve, and to divide each cottage into twelve shares. Cer-
tificates of ownership were given for these shares, transfer-
able through the Farm School Bank, which is another
feature of this enterprising little community. The whole
idea worked so well that in 1893 the superintendent of the
school issued a proclamation officially naming the playground settlement "Cottage Row" and announcing the various officers to be elected. After the election, a city hall, six
by ten feet was erected, soon followed by Audubon Hall, a
building used as a home for the pets of the boys. Any visitor
to the school who has witnessed an election at this little
island-city government never forgets the orderly example
of how politics should be run.

A disaster took place a few years after the Cottage Row
plan was begun, almost fifty years to the day since the

1842 tragedy. On Sunday afternoon, April 10, 1892, Instructor A. F. Nordberg had been attending church in South Boston, and ten picked boys left Thompson's Island by boat to bring him back to the school. Soon after 7 p.m., with the instructor safely on board, they began the return trip. At a point between Spectacle Island and Thompson's Island, evidently quite near the spot where the *Polka* had gone down half a century before, the sailboat struck a sudden squall and capsized. The eleven people clung to the bottom of the craft and waited for help. A tug steamed by; they shouted for assistance; but the night was getting dark and they were not noticed.

Back on the island, terribly worried by the prolonged absence of the boys, Superintendent Bradley was walking along the beach with his lantern. Some of the survivors told him afterward that they saw his figure, but he could not see them. He did notice a fire on an island far in the distance, and tried to pick up the silhouette of the boat against the background of the fire as he walked up and down, but his efforts were in vain. The water was cold, and as the night wore on the more exhausted boys, one by one, slipped into the water. By eleven o'clock there were only two boys left, O. W. Clement and C. A. Limb—a few minutes later the boat touched the beach at Spectacle Island. The tragic news was soon told; a boat was secured and rushed to Thompson's Island where Superintendent Bradley, already prepared for the worst, received the word that Nordberg and eight of the boys had drowned.

Another disaster of 1892 was witnessed by the boys at the school when the great balloon of Professor Rogers plunged into the water just off the island. Professor A. A. Rogers, Assistant Thomas Fenton, erstwhile employee of Austin & Stone's Museum, and Delos E. Goldsmith, a re-

porter, had taken off from Boston Common on the afternoon of July 4. A hundred thousand people were on the
Common, and a million others were watching the event
from nearby vantage points. It was Rogers' 118th ascension,
and he was full of confidence as the huge balloon rose into
the air and out over the Harbor. As the gas bag passed over
Castle Island, Rogers saw that he would soon be swept out
to sea, so he pulled at the safety valve. The valve would not
open. As he struggled with all his strength, the fabric above
the valve began to rip. It widened to a foot, then, a yard,
and the escaping gas almost overcame the three men. The
balloon dropped like a rock as the gas escaped. Boats from
all over the Harbor headed for the spot it must hit. Just
before the ship struck the water, Goldsmith released two
carrier pigeons from their cage. When the great bag crashed
into the ocean he was drawn under the sea. Rogers and
Goldsmith struck out for Thompson's Island, from which
the school boat had already started to go to the rescue.
Goldsmith was saved by the Farm School boys, but Rogers
had sunk beneath the waves before the boat reached him.
Fenton, entangled in the meshes of the net, was picked up in
an unconscious condition and died before he could be taken
to the hospital. Goldsmith recovered and was able to write
the story of the accident, while his brother Wallace illustrated the tale with some vivid sketches.

Charles Henry Bradley died in office on January 30, 1922.
Before he became sick, he had appointed Paul Francis
Swasey as supervisor of the school, and this young graduate
of the Massachusetts Institute of Technology now became
acting superintendent. The appointment became permanent
on February 18, 1923. He increased the number of classes
from four to six, thus making it possible for the boys graduating from the Farm and Trades School to enter the second

or third year of high school. Mr. Swasey resigned on November 30, 1926.

William Maxfield Meacham his successor, was installed in office under the first formal ceremony of its kind in the history of the school. It is of interest to note that the place of his birth, Hyde Park, Vermont, is within twenty miles of the birthplaces of his predecessors, Bradley and Swasey.

There have been three unusual bequests in the history of the school. The first was made by a Jewish philanthropist, Judah Touro, who had contributed to the fund used in building Bunker Hill Monument. His $5,000 donation was gratefully accepted. On his gravestone he ordered placed the information that he was the last "of my race."

Another gift to the school was that of John D. Williams, with the proviso that each year when the building was painted, pea-green paint, mixed by special formula, should be applied. The formula has been carefully preserved and every time the building was painted some pea-green paint was mixed in, and one of the Board of Managers took oath to the fact.

James Longley, one of the leading Boston bankers of his day, was not particularly interested in the Farm and Trades School until one day when he happened to see a student from the school. He was so impressed with the bearing of the boy that from that time on he became an ardent supporter of the institution, leaving the sum of $150,000 to the school in his will.

Among the students who attended school at what is now Thompson academy were Thomas J. Evans, a Civil War veteran; LeRoy S. Kenfield, with the Boston Symphony Orchestra for a third of a century; William Alcott, of the *Boston Globe;* Henry Fox, chief of the Boston Fire Department; marathon runner Clarence DeMar; Bob Emery of radio and television fame; Leslie Jones, *Boston Herald* photographer; and Cyrus Durgin of the *Boston Globe*.

Besides regular courses, the students have the practical experience of caring for and running the *Pilgrim*, the school boat of which all the boys are so proud.

Without question the groves of trees on Thompson's Island are not surpassed anywhere in Boston Harbor, and everyone connected with the school is justly proud of them. In 1846 Theodore Lyman imported four thousand larches and two thousand English oaks which he presented to the institution.

I have visited this island hundreds of times in the spring, summer, fall, and winter, and was conducted through all the various establishments. There are 108 students now at the academy. Under the able leadership of Mr. George Wright wonderful work is being done there. If the proud parent who raises one son to manhood is said to have done the community and his country a worthy service, think what we owe to this society, which has supplied fatherly interest and guidance to two thousand times this number. Thompson Academy at Thompson's Island is a splendid example of what can be done for the worthy boy of today.

On Thursday, February 18, 1971, a gigantic fire destroyed the administration building at Thompson Academy. Nevertheless, the academy will continue to function on the island. Until final arrangements are made, the spacious gymnasium and certain areas in the dormitories will be used for classes.

6

ISLANDS ALONG THE BACK CHANNEL

SPECTACLE ISLAND

Lying between Castle and Long Islands, the two cliffs of Spectacle Island occupy a commanding location in Boston Harbor. The earliest mention of this *pince-nez* island is in 1635, when it was included with Deer, Hog, and Long Islands for a total yearly rent of four shillings. The first known excitement took place three years later when thirty woodsmen were marooned here by the cold weather. Twelve of the men were later able to reach Governor's Island, but seven of them were carried on the ice out to the Brewster Islands where they remained for two days without food or fire. One woodcutter died, and many of the men had their arms and legs frozen.

In 1649 the town of Boston granted the island to planters for the small yearly rate of sixpence an acre, but the plan did not work out very well. Presently Thomas Bill, a lighterman, began to buy up the rights of the owners of Spectacle Island, and by January 25, 1681, had acquired thirty-five acres. Samuel Bill, his son, now bought his father's acres and together with what he purchased from other people, believed he owned the whole of the island. Samuel was a butcher by trade.

His claim was disputed by Josiah, the son of Wampatuck, but Bill straightway satisfied Josiah with "coin of the realm." Samuel Bill died on August 18, 1705, leaving the island to his widow with the provision that if she married she would lose two thirds of it. Less than a year later she married Eleazer Phillips, thus forfeiting most of the island to her son Samuel Bill, the younger. He acquired the rest of the land at her death.

After the inhabitants of Dorchester had protested against locating the proposed quarantine hospital at Squantum Neck, Spectacle Island was chosen as the site. On July 30, 1717, Samuel Bill and his wife Sarah sold a part of the Island for £100, and a suitable house was soon erected to receive the sick from incoming vessels.

Since ships coming from Ireland in 1729 carried smallpox, all Irish vessels arriving in Boston Harbor were required to discharge their passengers and crew at Spectacle Island Quarantine. A letter from William Beard to the selectmen of Boston, dated November 17, 1729, gives the reader some insight into the trials of the sea captain of that period. Beard, commander of the ship *Ann*, told the selectmen that he had brought his ship down to Spectacle Island from Ireland a month before and that "the Men and Passengers have thoroughly aired themselves so that now there is no danger of any infection being spread therefrom." He saw winter approaching and was anxious to start repairs so that the ship might again sail the high seas. His request was duly granted.

Wild animals have at various times lived on the islands in the Harbor, but very few have actually come to live there while they were occupied by white people. In 1725, however, so many bears were being killed around Boston that some of the beasts took to the ocean for refuge, several of them swimming across to Spectacle Island. Two were killed as they tried to escape, but only after a desperate struggle.

Samuel Bill, Jr., died on September 24, 1733, at his home on the island. Shortly afterward the selectmen of Boston believed another location was necessary for the Quarantine Station. On December 2, 1736, a committee reported that Rainsford's Island was available for this purpose. It seemed an ideal part of the Harbor, with deep waterways on each side of the island. A hospital was planned and commenced at Rainsford's, and by the end of 1737 it was ready for occupation. Spectacle Island, no longer needed by the city, was sold to Richard Bill in 1739.

In 1798 Joshua Henshaw was the only occupant of Spectacle Island, according to the census made that year. At this time the value of the buildings on the property was $200.

Two summer hotels were established at Spectacle Island, one run by a Mr. Woodroffe and the other by a Mr. Reed. A thriving business was enjoyed, but the existence of certain activities and games not allowed by the city of Boston brought police raiders in the year 1857, and from that time on the hotel business failed to prosper. The same year Nahum Ward paid $15,000 for the property, including two houses and two powder magazines similar to those at Governor's Island. One of these powder magazines is buried near the bridge of the nose on the low land. The history of these powder storerooms is unknown, as no one knows when they were built. A new edifice for the island was brought down on lighters by Mr. Ward from Boston.

Nahum Ward had a prosperous business of rendering dead horses and cattle. His son, Francis J. Ward, in 1882 said his work at Spectacle Island prevented many a plague in Boston, for if the dead animals had been allowed to stay in the city as long as three days, serious results might have followed.

In 1886 Joseph Marion moved to Spectacle from Long Island and built a cabin on the southern side of the cliff. Marion died in 1892, and his wife later married José Safarino, who had come to live at Spectacle Island in 1888. He had one son, José, aged eighteen, who made frequent visits over to Quarantine Rocks where he called on the jovial Grisiano Rio, otherwise known as Joe the Rock and Portuguese Joe.

The year 1898 had much excitement in store for the Safarino family. On April 24, during a severe blow, a catboat capsized right over Sculpin Ledge, half a mile from shore. José and his son rowed out in the gale and rescued the four men in the boat. One man was unconscious when picked up and died shortly afterward. That November brought the dreadful *Portland* Storm and the great four-masted steamship *Ohio* of the Wilson line went ashore close to their home. It was later pulled off.

Frank L. Murphy was born at Spectacle Island. The Reverend Mr. Hughes of Saint Mary's was rescued from drowning off the rocks of Spectacle Island by Frank Murphy's father. The Reverend Mr. Hughes was so grateful that he consecrated a chapel which Mr. Murphy constructed at the island, and for many years was a frequent visitor at the Murphy residence.

In 1892 the garbage reclaiming plant was located at Moon Island. Twenty years later, on April 12, 1912, the establishment was moved over to Spectacle Island and became known as the Boston Development and Sanitary Company, with Mr. Cranford in charge. In 1922 the contract was given to the Coleman Disposal Company and ten years later it was again awarded to this firm. Garbage from Boston added five acres to the size of the island, but this activity has stopped. The rendering business of the Ward Plant gradually dropped off, and not for many years have dead horses and cows been brought to this plant.

Just after the turn of the century four range lights were erected, but with the widening and straightening of the main channel, the lights were found unnecessary and demolished. Mr. Creed was keeper, remaining at the lights for over twenty years. He was succeeded by Captain Lelan Hart who came from Boston Light in 1926.

A little red school house was for many years the center of activity for the children of the island. Miss Ann MacWilliams was the last teacher in this building, coming to the island in 1916. Her final class was held in September 1933. At that time the pupils were Marion Timmons, Neal Haskins, and Helen Lescovitz.

We visited the island on Sunday, August 9, 1934, and spent the entire day rambling about the farm, lighthouses, and the two refineries. Walking toward José Safarino's cottage on the southern cliff, we reached the hut just as night was coming on. Safarino invited us in, and we sat down at his table. Lighting his lantern, he spun story after story of his childhood in the Harbor, telling how he played around the guns at Long Island Head as a child. He also spoke of his service aboard the lighthouse tender *Mayflower*, and of the rescue in 1898 which earned him the Massachusetts Humane Society's medal.

As the evening wore on, the time came to go back to our boat, so we bade farewell to this island fisherman. He warned us against the dangers of the garbage dump, where the rats grew as large as cats. We were lucky, however, to

encounter the night watchman of the island, George Low-
ther, who guided us along the road, keeping the great ro-
dents away with his flashlight. We reached our boat without
further incident.

The lifeless remains of Lynn Kauffman, a passenger on
the freighter *Utrecht,* washed ashore at Spectacle Island on
September 19, 1959. Accused of her murder, Radio Opera-
tor Van Rie of the *Utrecht* was later acquitted in a sensa-
tional trial.

The schooner *Snetind* was at the island from 1936 until
1951, when she was towed out to sea and sunk.

THIMBLE, CAT, AND HALF-MOON ISLANDS

Between Thompson's Island and the mainland there is a
small ledge the size of a house-lot which the government
chart honors by calling Thimble Island. It is a very appro-
priate name as it is a diminutive island.

Two other islands, formerly much larger than the area
the Government Chart indicates for Thimble Island, have
disappeared from the waters of the Harbor. Cat Island, located in Town River Bay is only mentioned twice in history. It was the home of one John Bond, a native of Boston,
who gave a mortgage for it sometime before 1700. Some
years later Joseph Palmer, the patriot, sold it to James
Brackett. Since it has now been dug up and taken away as
filling material, it is quite probable there will be no occasion for further historical research.

Half-Moon Island, however, has figured a little more in
the history of the period. It was formerly a fishing and
hunting center for nearby residents. On April 7, 1806, at a

town meeting in Quincy, it was voted to abandon the restriction respecting fishing and fowling on this island.

Colonel John Quincy once lived at Wollaston where he often entertained his friends, and traditions have come down to the present time of his famous strawberry parties given at Half-Moon Island before the top of "that now submerged gravel ridge" had been wholly washed away. When the Moon Island sewer was put in, much of the earth needed to construct the strandway out to the Head was taken from Half-Moon Island.

HANGMAN'S ISLAND

Hangman's Island is the next subject of our tour. It was often used in Colonial days as a source of slate material, Mrs. Olive Smallpiece owning the slate rights in the last part of the seventeenth century. One day Aaron Ingraham and Joseph Rayner went to the island to get a load of slate which Mrs. Smallpiece claimed was already cut. When they arrived and found that there was no cut stone, the men were forced to go over to Squantum to hire the services of William Green, a stone-splitter, before going to Hough's Neck to take in the slate.

For some unknown reason, the town of Quincy never claimed Hangman's Island, and the Commonwealth of Massachusetts took it over years ago. The regulations under which it may be leased prevented construction of a house or shack of any sort, but many fishermen disregarded the rules and built small service sheds in which they lived and stored their traps and seines. Matthew Powell on the ninth of January, 1878, asked permission to occupy the island, and ten years later Charles D. Daggett leased the acre of land for fifty dollars a year. About this time the dredging companies dumped mud dug from the channel into the area near Hangman's Island, so that there are now flats about the island.

On January 1, 1896, William J. Greenfield leased the island, continuing to occupy it until the First World War. After the war Stewart C. Woodworth lived here for three years. G. R. Maertins leased the island for a gunning stand in 1929, but his permit expired in 1930 and was not renewed. At present there is no occupant there. While canoeing in December 1934 we were marooned there for several hours when the wind reached gale force. In the lull which occurred about five o'clock that afternoon we headed for Long Island, where we were rescued by Captain Wilbur Bryant in the *Hilda E.* of the Winthrop Yacht Club.

MOON ISLAND

Moon Island, now connected to the mainland by the earth and gravel brought here from Half-Moon Island, was formerly called Manning's Moone, and in 1656 was valued at twenty-eight pounds. John Holland owned the Island around 1665, and when he died the estate was sold to Henry Ashhurst. The great sewer to Moon Island was begun in 1878, and for many years has been emptying into Boston Harbor. The only recorded excitement here was during the Revolution, when a Continental soldier was killed on the Head during one of the Harbor skirmishes.

Moon Island is the present site for revolver practice for the police. The firemen practice in putting out oil blazes here.

NUT ISLAND

The first mention we can find of Nut Island is on August 5, 1680, when Obediah Walker sold two thirds of the island to Richard Harris. At this time the island was also called Hoffs Thumb, because it was off the shore from Hoffs Neck, now known as Hough's Neck.

In 1793 a driftway for cattle was constructed between Nut Island and the mainland at Hough's Neck, and it was off this same driftway seventy-two years later that Marcus Cram met his death. The cattle run was covered at high tide by about seven feet of water. Cram and his family had driven over to Nut Island at low tide when the bar was bare. When they started to go back to the mainland he believed it was not too deep for his horse, but the animal, becoming confused in the current, ran the buggy off the driftway into deep water, and the family was soon struggling in the Bay. William H. Mears saw the accident from shore and saved all the occupants except Cram, who had gone down before Mears reached the scene.

A few years later the Federal Government started a testing ground for the heavy ordnance which was built at the Alger Foundry in South Boston. An epochal event of the period took place in October 1876, when a projectile weighing over five hundred pounds hit the Prince's Head target almost a mile away so hard that it penetrated completely through the twelve-inch plates of solid wrought iron. Another test a little later might have ended disastrously had not the shell cleared Prince's Head target by several hundred feet and buried itself in the graveyard at Hull.

The road connecting Nut Island and Hough's Neck is

now well above the high-water mark, permitting automobiles to drive out and around the island.

A little incident which Morton of Merrymount tells concerning his servant Bubbles and Nut Island will close our survey of what was once known as Hoffs Thumb.

"Bubbles and hee goes in the Canow to Nut-Island for Brants, and there his host makes a shotte and breakes the winges of many. Bubbles in hast and single handed, paddels out lik a Cow in cage; his host calls back to rowe two handed like to a pare of oares, and before this could be performed, the fowles had time to swimme to other flockes, and so to escape; the best part of the pray being lost, mayd his host to mutter at him, and so to parte for that time discontended."

7

GOVERNOR'S, APPLE, AND
SNAKE ISLANDS

As the visitor to Boston sailed up the main ship channel in 1945 to pass Deer Island Light on his way to the pier, he would notice three islands, each in turn larger than the other, on the starboard side of the boat. They were Snake, Apple, and Governor's Islands, long connected with the history of our Bay. Snake Island had scarcely three acres, Apple Island claimed nine, while Governor's Island has seventy-two acres intact from the ravages of the sea. Two of the three islands have vanished, while the third has undergone radical changes.

GOVERNOR'S ISLAND

Governor's Island had without question more unofficial visitors than any other Boston island in the past generation. Hundreds of boats from South Boston, Charlestown, East Boston, and Winthrop called here every year. As far as casual visitors are concerned, it is safe to say it was the best-known island in all New England.

A quarter century ago, as we made our way up the Harbor, we passed close to the green, hilly shores of the isle, and its beauty always held our attention. Rounding the southern point, we noticed the demilune battery on the shore, and dropped anchor near the ruined granite wharf. Then we rowed ashore to land on the sandy beach. We were then near the site of the home of John Winthrop, the first Puritan occupant of the Island.

The year 1945 was the last which saw Governor's Island resembling in any way the days when the island was first active as a fort.

Roger Conant owned Conant's Island, as it was first called, while he was a resident of Nantasket. According to his statement of June 2, 1671, he had been a planter in New England "these 48 years and three months" and had been with the first, he believed the very first, to live in "this wilderness." Conant is regarded by John Wingate Thornton as the first actual governor of Massachusetts. Roger Conant later moved to Salem, and then to Beverly where he died at the age of eight-six. Although we have no actual record to prove that he lived on the island, it is reasonable to believe that he spent some of his life here.

The struggles of the Court of Massachusetts concerning the leasing of the island to John Winthrop form a unique part of the records of Massachusetts Bay. Before Winthrop was awarded the property it had been appropriated for "publique benefits and uves" on July 5, 1631. Exactly twenty-four days later it somewhat belied this purpose when the ship *Friendship* ran aground here on its way to the Christopher Islands. Not quite a year later, the entire island was "demised to John Winthrop, Esq., the psent Goun^r, for the terme of his life, for the ffine of fforty shillings, & att the yearely rent of xij$d$." John Winthrop promised to plant a vineyard and an orchard here, and in return his heirs were to be allowed the island for twenty-one years, provided they paid one fifth part of all fruits and profits to the Court. The Government reserved the right to take the island away from the heirs if they failed to improve the property. Conant's Island was called Governor's Garden this same year.

Certain changes were made in the agreement between Winthrop and the Court on March 4, 1635, whereby the rent was made a "hogshead of the best wine that shall growe there, to be paid yearely, after the death of the said John Winthrop, and noething before." The vineyard did so poorly, however, that the Court decided to take no chances with the future, so on May 12, 1640, the rent was again changed, this time to two bushels of apples every year. As this was to be paid during his lifetime, John Winthrop made the first payment on the seventh of October, 1640. The Winthrop family probably continued this yearly payment until 1683, for at that time Adam Winthrop petitioned to be allowed to make a final cash settlement. The Court granted his request, allowing him to send "fiue pounds money fortuith, by the first opportunity, to our agents in England."

In January 1642 a very peculiar accident occurred just off the island. Three men, sailing a shallop from Braintree, were approaching Castle Island when the sail had to be shortened. One of them, in stepping forward, caught his foot on a fowling piece which had a French lock. The firearm exploded, shooting him in the thigh, while the man in the stern received forty shots in his chest. The third man, unharmed by the explosion, was able to bring the boat to Governor's Island, where the injured men were attended. Both wounded men eventually recovered.

President Henry Dunster of Harvard was a property owner in Boston Harbor at one time. John Winthrop, in 1641, granted Governor's Island to Dunster and Captain George Cooke, provided they turned the property over to Adam Winthrop and Elizabeth Glover on the occasion of this couple's marriage. John Winthrop, however, reserved for himself one third of all the grapes, apples, pears, and plums that might grow there. This orchard was probably the first in the Colony.

In our chapter on Castle Island we mention the arrival of Monsieur La Tour, the French Huguenot, at Boston Harbor, and the incident concerning La Tour, Winthrop, and Mrs. Gibbons on the beach at Governor's Island. Let us go on from that point. After inviting La Tour and Mrs. Gibbons to supper, Winthrop sent the lady home in his own boat and went up to town with the Frenchman. La Tour was lodged at Captain Gibbons' house in Boston, and the next day the colonists discussed just what they should do about the request of La Tour for men and ships to fight D'Aulnay, La Tour's Catholic enemy. The Puritans told La Tour that they would not object to his hiring men in the colony, but informed the Huguenot they were forced to withhold their official approval.

On July 14, 1643, La Tour left Boston Harbor with a fleet of six vessels, including his own, and on arriving at Saint John engaged in a short skirmish with D'Aulnay. The next year La Tour again came to Boston but as D'Aulnay meanwhile had sent a committee to wait upon the governor, the Puritans cooled considerably toward La Tour's proposals, dismissing him with a small quantity of commodities and a vessel. La Tour repaid the trusting colonists by seizing the ship lent him and putting the Boston men on shore near Cape Sable. Perhaps the final point to remember in the whole affair is that when D'Aulnay died in 1651, La Tour married his wife!

Adam Winthrop leased Governor's Island to Sir Thomas Temple in 1669 for twenty-one pounds, and Temple in turn rented it to William Towers and John Kind, Boston butchers, for thirty pounds. Temple left for England soon after the transaction, and in his absence Governor's Island changed hands. Nicholas Salisbury was a tenant of John Keer who leased the island in 1700 from John Richard, the American agent of Sir Thomas Temple.

Ann Winthrop became heir to Governor's Island shortly after 1700. Although Sweetser tells us that in 1696 an eight-gun battery had been constructed on the southeastern point and a ten-gun battery erected on the southwestern point, no batteries were actually built there till much later. Ann Winthrop was notified in 1744 that the Government had decided to erect a battery at the eastern shore. From the speech of Governor William Shirley to the House of Representatives on October 10, 1744, we learn that:

"A Committee of your House have been with me to view a proper Place on *Governor's Island* for erecting a Battery to prevent the Enemy's landing on the back side of it, which would expose the Works at Castle William to their Bombs, and have, I suppose, treated with the proprietor about purchasing Land there for that Use."

On October 19, 1744, a bill for this purpose was passed, and five days later five hundred pounds was appropriated for a block house and two batteries to be placed at Governor's Island. Three acres of the land were purchased from Ann Winthrop for the fort.

An aftermath of the capture of Louisburg in 1745 was the incident of the deserving watchman. Governor Shirley told John Day, a tenant at Governor's Island, to guard the

Harbor against any vessels arriving in port just before the fleet started for the Canadian expedition. Day and night for six months he watched the Harbor, even hiring others to help him. The work cost John Day fifty pounds in addition to "Arms Powder & Ball Lignori and Provisions for all those who watch'd." On December 9, 1749, the House of Representatives ordered that Day be paid the sum of 24 £ 10 s 9d in full consideration for his service. Phipps, who was then governor of Massachusetts, approved the settlement the House had made with Day.

A number of people were born at Governor's Island during the three centuries of occupation by white men. An outstanding privateer, David Williams, was born near the site of the present ruined wharf back in 1759, and his exploits in Boston Harbor and Massachusetts Bay were long remembered by those who knew him.

The Revolutionary War came and went without disturbing the tranquil sleep of the island that Roger Conant once owned, and only one incident of note can be connected with the birth of our Nation. On March 5, 1776, five of Lord Percy's transport ships were driven ashore at Governor's Island in a great gale that completely thwarted the British in their plans for overcoming the Americans at Dorchester Heights.

Ten years after the Treaty of Paris the Massachusetts Historical Society, at the invitation of James Winthrop, held a regularly scheduled meeting near the site of John Winthrop's house. After the minutes of the meeting were read and the business discussed, the group enjoyed a walk around the island. It would be a delightful event if some historical society of today should meet at one of our Harbor islands.

The Massachusetts Direct Tax Census of 1798 lists Governor's Island as having only one dwelling, Josiah Mason being the occupant and James Winthrop the owner. At that time the island's value was placed at $500, but no mention is made of the guard house or the batteries. On the ninth of April, 1808, the Government purchased from James Winthrop one acre of land at the southern point and three acres on the summit, together with a road forty feet wide between the two. The purchase price was $15,000. The fort was named for Joseph Warren.

On May 23, 1808, the demilune battery was begun on the southern point by Lieutenant Sylvanus Thayer, who is known as the "Father of West Point." Thayer also erected the four-star fortress at the top of the hill and the dungeon keep which was built on the same spot prior to the Civil War. The genius of this young officer has never been fully appreciated by the residents of Massachusetts, and it is believed that the greatest engineer which the army has ever produced should have some recognition for his work.

On the wall of the Bostonian Society office at the Old State House there is a view taken from Beacon Hill. This sketch shows the home of the Sea-Fencibles, a low one-story building erected over the water of what was formerly Back Bay. This organization, which included many prominent Bostonians, possibly caused the British to give up the idea of capturing Boston. The Sea-Fencibles arranged giant furnaces on the demilunes at Governor's Island for heating iron, shot, and tar to be thrown onto the British ships by mortars. Artist Robert Salmon painted this Governor's Island scene at the demilune more than a century and a quarter ago.

The 1814 Treaty of Ghent ended our last war with England, and Governor's Island lapsed into the pastoral state it normally enjoyed. Even the announcement in 1833 that it

would lose the name of Fort Warren to George's Island
farther down the Harbor did not seem to matter, especially
when the new title would honor the first governor of Massachusetts, John Winthrop.

The zigzag stairway going down to the demilune battery
was installed in 1852, and the dungeon keep was begun
about the same time. The keystone of the arch placed over
one of the short tunnels gives us the date when the works
were finally completed, 1872.

We would like to be able to say that many splendid regiments were quartered here from time to time during the
Civil War, but such was not the case. Only a skeleton garrison was ever at Fort Winthrop. Various state organizations
stationed here were terribly bored with the monotony of
the work. In the fall of 1863 General Schouler inspected the
fortification and noticed there were thirty-six guns on the
island. Sometime before 1892 the graves of the soldiers at
Fort Warren were transferred to Governor's Island, and in
that year the graves of the men at Castle Island were also
brought over. The graveyard stood on the northern slope of
the hill, possibly two hundred yards from the keep. Every
grave was again moved in 1908, this time to Deer Island.

After an attempt at garrisoning the Fort had been made
during the Spanish-American War, the island returned to
the caretaking status it usually enjoyed. Among the caretakers who have made Fort Winthrop their home since 1880
are the following sergeants: Roche, Schwartz, Neeves,
Shaw, Geyer, Peterson, and Benjamin. Sergeant Benjamin,
a West Indian Negro who retired and returned to Jamaica,
was killed in the great tornado there. Sergeant Shaw had
come to Governor's Island from Castle Island in May 1901,
bringing his wife and two sons with him. Nothing unusual
took place until September 1902. On the seventh day of

that month, a Sunday, there were several hundred people visiting the island. The other resident of the island had taken a trip to the mainland; Shaw was quite busy warning people away from the various stores of powder hidden in the earthern mounds.

Late that afternoon, three men landed from a fishing boat at the demilune battery located near the bottom of the zigzag stairway and matched coins to see which of them would stay to watch the boat. The three men were Albert Cotton of Somerville, and Joseph Wakefield and Christian Knudson of South Boston. Knudson lost the toss, stayed behind to watch the boat, and thereby saved his life. The other two men climbed the stairs leading up to the path that winds about the entire southern side of the upper level. Soon Knudson could see them near a powder magazine. Cotton sat down on top of the mound and started to smoke his pipe. Wakefield went around to the front of the magazine, and that was the last time he was ever seen. In a moment there was a terrific concussion and Boston felt its worst explosion. Knudson saw Cotton being blown through the air. The whole top of the island seemed to rise. Bricks, granite blocks weighing tons, earth, and stones were scattered all over the island. Knudson was struck by a rock and knocked unconscious.

There had been eighteen thousand pounds of gunpowder stored in regular hundred-pound barrels inside the powder magazine, and in some way it had been ignited. Wakefield was blown to pieces, only a part of his body ever being found. Cotton was found many yards from the scene of the explosion, frightfully mutilated, and died without regaining consciousness. All over the island various groups had miraculous escapes from the giant stones that landed among them. The Saint Joseph's Athletic Association of the

West End had been picnicking when the blast went off, and the debris landed all around them. When they discovered that no one was seriously hurt, the entire group knelt in grateful prayer on the slopes of the hillside.

The explosion did considerable damage on the island, and even out in the Harbor two boats were struck by rocks from the blast. The senior four-oared shell of the Jeffries Point Athletic Association was sunk by a boulder, and a rowboat coming from East Boston was struck and quickly filled. Passing boats saved the occupants, none of whom was injured. Windows in Lynn and Winthrop were shattered, Castle Island was badly damaged, and plate-glass windows on Atlantic Avenue in Boston were smashed. The old castle itself was struck by two granite slabs that can still be seen at the base of the fortress. Four girls, who were trapped in the short tunnel that stands at the head of the zigzag stairway, were horribly frightened when several huge granite rocks came tumbling in beside them, but they were not hurt.

Sergeant Shaw's residence was down on the lower plain of the island between the wharf and the 1808 shore battery. His younger son, Hugh, who was playing the piano at the time of the explosion, was thrown to the floor by the shock. The boy rushed out of doors to see that the explosion had actually pushed the tide away from the beach scores of feet, and that a heavy black smoke hung over the entire island.

On the way to the scene of the explosion, Hugh found terrorized groups huddled together in various parts of the fort, wondering what the next moment would bring. The boy hurried on and reached the scene of the blast. He saw Cotton's body and started to help the others look for Wakefield. Another man was found, apparently badly hurt, but after examination it was seen he was only extremely intoxicated. Shaw told the writer in July 1935, that he could never understand why at least a dozen people were not killed by the blast with so many passing and repassing the powder magazine. He also spoke of the terrible feeling he had the next day when his father had him go into the adjacent powder magazine to count the barrels of gunpowder. Shaw was relieved when he completed his count and came out into the sunlight again.

Although it was believed by the investigators that either Wakefield or Cotton set off the explosion, later a new version of the story appeared. I cannot vouch for its accuracy, but it was told to me by a man who has a reputation for truthfulness. He told me that the disaster was caused by twelve boys from East Boston who had broken into the powder magazine to take three hundred-pound kegs of explosives. Breaking open the small barrels, they sprinkled a trail of powder along the path and over to an empty magazine, where the boldest boy scratched a match and applied it to the trail. The method was quite similar to that employed by the British when they blew up Boston Light in 1776. According to this story, the boys, amazed to find that the powder blazed up, were panic stricken. Terrified by the thought of what they had done, they rushed to the back of the abandoned magazine. Meanwhile the blaze was eating its way along the trail, and in a moment the terrific concussion threw the boys against the walls. A few minutes later they dragged their way down to their boat, and soon left the scene of their crime. For thirty years, according to this version, the real story of the explosion remained an enigma, but with the death of the ringleader it could now be told.

The guns on the island were taken down behind the large barn at the fortress, where they were broken up by dynamite, and the fort was soon afterward practically abandoned. Thus closed the active part in the history of

Governor's Island. Although Sergeant Shaw remained at the island some time longer, the task of keeping hundreds of people in order was too much for any one individual, and in March 1905 the army removed the caretaker.

The War Department now gave the city of Boston permission to make certain improvements at Governor's Island. In 1911, since nothing had been done, Major-General Frederick D. Grant wrote Mayor Fitzgerald criticizing the city for its neglect. In the same year the Lighthouse Department, thwarted in its efforts to use Castle Island for its base, tried to obtain Governor's Island, thinking it a suitable location. The city of Boston, however, was taking steps for a proposed park at the island, and had already chosen Arthur A. Shurtleff, prominent landscape architect, to draw elaborate plans for the beautification of the property. The Lighthouse Department finally gave up its attempts to gain the island and moved to Chelsea.

The next spring work began on a long flight of broad granite stairs and a gravel walk leading up from the dock. The wide, granite stairs were completed, and then the entire plan was abandoned because of friction with the Government.

Between the time the Government removed the ordnance-sergeant from Governor's Island and the year the new stairs were put in, two individuals had gained a somewhat dubious possession of the seventy acres of terrain. They were John Barnacle and Sala Brown, who were staying at the island in a "quasi-hermitical" state. Although they lived separately at first, each occupying a deserted powder magazine on different sides of the island, they later decided on a merger and moved into an archway having two small powder storerooms. Barnacle and Brown lived on the clams from the flats and fish from the water with an occasional dinner of vegetables. Once a month one of them took the dory and rowed to East Boston with two bushels of clams which he exchanged for a bag of potatoes and other supplies. When in 1912 the Park Department began their active work on the island, these two men were forced to seek another location to carry on their peaceful pursuit of happiness.

An alarming note was seen in the announcement by the City Board of Health on July 24, 1913, that the large well at Governor's Island was a source of typhoid fever. The board recommended that it be cleaned out and properly protected against contamination. A cover was made for the well, and as late as 1931 the water remained pure.

After the First World War the Navy took over Governor's Island, assuming control December 1, 1922. Since the Navy never used the property, in 1930 Mayor James M. Curley included it in his scheme for a great Boston airport. Because of technical restraints placed on the city by the Government, plans were not carried out, although the airport almost reached the island even then. On August 6, 1935, Governor Curley made a special request of the Federal Government to expend a million dollars to connect the airport and the island.

The islands in winter are always astonishing revelations of Jack Frost at his best. We have visited many of the deserted islands just after a heavy snowstorm when the scenery itself was well worth a long journey from the fireside on a winter's day. Perhaps the most enjoyable trip we ever made was on February 1, 1935. At that time we walked across the ice from the East Boston Airport and up the slopes of Governor's Island. Two boys were skiing down the side of the island. Over by the southern powder magazines we found a drift eighteen feet high and twenty feet wide. At one place, right under the keystone of the arch that reads "1872," the passageway was almost buried from view.

Governor's Island also has its legends and ghost stories. The legends tell us that at one time a chain stretched across the Harbor from Castle Island to Governor's Island. Several small boys have recently assured me that there is still in existence a tunnel which goes under the Harbor from Governor's Island to Castle Island. Of course, there is no truth in either story. We must blame John Winthrop for one of the ghost stories. On the eighteenth of January, 1644, three men sailing into Boston saw weird lights arise out of the water between the city and Governor's Island. The lights shot out sparkles and flames and then took the form of a man. A weird voice was heard calling: "Boy, boy, come away, come away." Winthrop believed that it was the spirit of the sailor who had blown up Captain Chaddock's pinnace, as the sailor's body was never found.

We shall continue our journey around Governor's Island in the year 1945. Climbing the Park Department's wide granite stairway, we cross a path, flanked by massive green mounds, which leads in both directions around the island. There are twenty-four of these mounds containing the powder magazines, with seven on the lower level of the fort. Reaching the end of the granite stairway, we go through fields, underbrush, and shrubbery until we stand near the old dungeon keep itself. I always like to call it a "castle," as it was formerly entered by a drawbridge over a moat and surely is picturesque enough to be classed with the strongholds of ancient times.

We go down the granite stairs on each side of the two-hundred-foot tunnel, noticing the original entrance to the old castle high above the level of the dry moat. When the snowdrifts extended almost halfway up to the entrance in 1934, the more adventursome boys from Winthrop jumped down from the entrance into the drift. The only way into the fort is through the western side of the cellar, where two of the musketry loopholes have been widened. While squeezing our large frames through the broken musketry loopholes, we think of the Civil War days at Fort Warren when six men forced their way out of similar holes that had not been widened at all!

We are now in the dark cellar, and if you haven't brought your flashlight, you would be wise to go up the stairs to the upper level at once. Stalactites point down from the ceiling; a cool, damp atmosphere pervades the entire cellar. We who have lights will explore the various ghostlike chambers of the lower level, visiting one small room in particular. It is a dungeon hard to find and we must follow directions carefully to reach our goal. First we make sure that we are in the outside room of the northern side of the dungeon keep. Then, with our faces due south, we walk straight ahead out of the doorway and should soon find the entrance to the dungeon. Inside it is always pitch dark, so we must be cautious. The granite upright in the middle of the dungeon was the post around which prisoners were handcuffed. After a few days spent here the most hardened criminal was probably willing to behave.

Continuing our explorations, we notice the great brick cistern where the water supply was kept. Let us go up the circular granite staircase, the pride of its builder, Sylvanus Thayer. Stopping at the courtyard on the first floor, we view with mingled feelings the ruin caused by the vandals of Boston. These lovers of destruction have done a thorough job of tearing down the inside of the building, but most of its charm can still be appreciated. Where officers and men formerly paraded we now see only pitiful piles of granite and brick, forever separated from their former grandeur and usefulness. Resuming our climb, we reach the second floor. In 1927 the thrill seeker could work his way around the entire story, balancing on beams and jumping from one window ledge to another. But now there is only a small part of the floor left, comprising the hallway and a small apartment facetiously designated "Mabel's Room," thereby dating the time of this christening as contemporary with the farce, *Up in Mabel's Room*. A dangerous opening in the floor of the hallway makes us careful as we step across to stand at the old entrance. As a boy was killed here in 1930, we shall be very cautious as we move about.

We now ascend the next flight and reach the top of the keep. Here we notice the sixteen emplacements where formerly the great guns overlooked the Harbor. A wall six feet wide surrounds the roof of the fortress where at one time the huge Parrott guns were sentinels. The roof was for many years covered by a wooden shelter built to shield the big guns. We jump up on the wall, keeping a respectful distance from its sloping edge and look out over the Harbor. One of the prettiest views of the Bay is from the top of this castle. Eighteen towns and cities can be seen from this vantage point, while over fifty localities can easily be identified with the aid of a telescope.

Ocean liners sweep majestically by on their way to Europe, small pleasure yachts run in and out among the neighboring islands, and sturdy tugs with their barges puff along down the Bay. The drone of an airplane high above the castle is in striking contrast to the peaceful scenes on the island itself. Castle Island is directly across the Harbor, its green banks dotted with people. There the white monument of granite to Donald McKay and his clipper ships stands out distinctly against the duller gray of Boston's oldest fortress. To the right we see the giant drydock where formerly the *Leviathan* was annually overhauled. The Custom House, the Federal Building, and the Shoe Machinery

Building are prominent in Boston's skyline, while around in the northwest Bunker Hill monument adds its silhouette. Off to the east the Winthrop Water Tower and the Deer Island Prison are outstanding landmarks, and far in the distance Graves Light and Boston Light are seen. Around to the southeast Long Island Light and the buildings of the Long Island Hospital add their beauty, while the incinerator at Spectacle Island gives a somewhat dubious note to the vista. Thompson's Island, the home of the Farm and Trades School, completes the delightful view from the top of the old castle. But the sun is getting low in the west, and we must soon leave.

We begin our trip back to the beach by passing through the long tunnel, making a right turn, and walking by three of the empty powder magazines. The third magazine was the one in which young Hugh Shaw counted the powder barrels on September 8, 1902. We now reach the scene of the worst explosion in the history of Boston. Although the contours have been somewhat softened in the thirty-three years that have intervened since that Sunday afternoon, even now we can see evidence of the catastrophe. The floor of the magazine is still in position, but the huge blocks are scattered about all over the island. We go down the short tunnel where the four girls hid at that time, climbing over the same blocks which almost crushed them, and descend the curious zigzag stairway, to the water battery on the beach.

After walking along the shore until we are back at the ruined wharf, we get into our tender and row to the ship. And so we say goodby to Governor's Island of 1945 and steer our way out into the Harbor. The entire Governor's Island was flattened out in 1946 and 1947 and is now an active part of the Logan International Airport.

APPLE ISLAND

Again we step back to the year 1945. The tree at Apple Island is exactly a mile from the castle at Governor's, but our route of a quarter century ago by boat is much longer. We must stay in the main channel, sailing about three miles before we are able to anchor in "Apple Island Road," a point between the Cottage Park Yacht Club and the island. Although the flats around Apple Island make it a dangerous place at low tide, proper observance of the buoys will prevent a disastrous ending to our trip. The landing in 1945 should be made on the Winthrop side, near the site of William Marsh's wharf opposite old Chelsea Point.

The first prominent owner of Apple Island was the Honorable Thomas Hutchinson, father of Governor Thomas Hutchinson, who wrote an admirable history of early Massachusetts. In 1724 Hutchinson sold the island to Estes Hatch for the equivalent of $1000. When the Hatch estate was settled in 1760, James Mortimer purchased the Island for £133 6s. 8d., but Mortimer lived only thirteen years longer. By his will his wife Hannah received half of the island's income while the other half went to James's brother, Peter Mortimer. Some idea of the extensive farm there may be gathered from the inventory included in the Mortimer will, part of which follows:

Apple Island, so called in Boston Harbor, with the buildings thereon,	£200
About ten ton of hay,	15
An old mare, £6; mare colt 2 years old £10	16
A horse colt 10 weeks old,	3
A dray cart, 10s; a hand cart 10s,	1

A provision in the will decreed that should Peter Mortimer die before James's widow, the island should go to Philip Mortimer of Connecticut. What actually happened is quite unusual. Hannah Mortimer died only three days after her husband, and Peter passed away the following day. This, however, turned the island away from the male line of Mortimers so that Mary Mortimer, Peter's widow, became the owner of Apple Island. Shurtleff suggests that she probably erected the three gravestones in Copp's Hill Burial Ground in grateful recognition of her three beneficient relatives.

Mary Mortimer married Daniel Waters, reserving the island for her brother Joseph Wilcox, who lived in Waterford, Ireland. The Revolutionary War came, and the Continental troops probably raided the farm there, taking off cattle and sheep to use for troops at Cambridge. Following the war, and nineteen years after the Treaty of Paris, Mary Wilcox Mortimer Waters died. Joseph Wilcox thus came to own Apple Island, although his residence was three thousand miles away. When Wilcox died, the island came into the possession of his son Robert, who moved to Northumberland, England.

We shall now change the scene of our story to Germantown, Quincy. William Marsh and his family came to live in Germantown about the year 1812. He was a quiet Englishman, called by many a "remittance man," as he received money from home at regular intervals. Something turned the inhabitants against Mr. Marsh and his family, so that he was requested to leave town. Marsh had always loved the water, and during his sojourn at Germantown had grown to admire our beautiful Harbor. When his neighbors asked him to leave, he bought a ten-ton sailboat and left Germantown with all his worldly possessions aboard.

Marsh purchased the boat about the first of May, 1814, and cruised all about the Harbor, stopping at Hog Island until John Breed requested him to leave. Among other places he visited was Apple Island. When the chilling blasts of November winds made him think of a home for the winter, he remembered the snug colonial mansion of the Mortimers at this island, so he landed and took possession of the uninhabited house. By the time spring came he was firmly established, and since he was contented in his new home, he tried to find its owner. But as Robert Wilcox was three thousand miles away, it was not until many years had passed that he was reached. Marsh agreed to pay $550 for the island, and on on January 15, 1830, the final papers were passed.

Marsh visited Boston once a year, appearing on State Street to discuss the various events of the period. Quite often he was seen at Point Shirley, where he purchased most of his needed provisions. But wherever he went, his manner and bearing were mysterious, and to his death he was looked upon as a very odd character. He died on the island on November 22, 1833, and was buried on the western slope near his old home. His mansion was destroyed by fire on November 11, 1835.

Oliver Wendell Holmes was inspired to write his *Island Ruin* about William Marsh of Apple Island. I quote a few lines from the poem:

> *They told strange things of that mysterious man;*
> *Believe who will, deny them such as can;*
> *Why should we fret if every passing sail*
> *Had its old seamen talking on the rail?*
> *His birthplace England, as his speech might show*
> *Or his hale cheek, that wore the red streak's glow*

He lived at ease beneath his elm-trees' shade
Did naught for gain, yet all his debts were paid;
They said his house was framed with curious cares,
Lest some old friend might enter unawares;
That on the platform of his chamber's door
Hinged a loose square that opened through the floor;
Touch the black silken tassel next the bell,
Down with a crash, the flapping trapdoor fell;
Three stories deep the falling wretch would strike,
To writhe at leisure on a boarder's pike.
Why tell each idle guess, each whisper vain?
Enough; the scorched and cindered beams remain.
He came, a silent pilgrim to the West,
Some old-world mystery throbbing in his breast;
Close to the thronging mart he lived alone;
He lived; he died. The rest is all unknown.

Marsh's daughters attracted many young men from the nearby mainland, and the girls married into the better families of what was formerly called Pullen Point. There are today many descendants of William Marsh living in the town of Winthrop.

Apple Island was sold to the city of Boston by Edward T. Marliave on May 21, 1867, for $3,750. Sweetser mentions many of the ships that have been burned on the shores of the Island, including the *Ontario*, the *Baltic*, and the *James Adger*.

The last two craft to be burned at Apple Island were the *Coyote* and the *Hen and Chickens* lightship.

When the Portuguese settlers were ordered to leave Long Island, they scattered all over the Harbor, two or three families choosing Apple Island on which to establish their homes. Joseph King, one of the Portuguese who moved there, was soon made the official representative at the island of the

Board of Street Commissioners of Boston, under whose jurisdiction the property remained. Unfortunately for King,
the belligerent element of the city soon found that Apple
Island was an ideal place to engage in fistic combats, and
the neighboring town of Winthrop protested against the
uproar, which could be heard there every Sunday. The city
of Boston sent Patrolmen Emil S. Liemann and T. T. Mc-
Carthy down to the island on August 25, 1901, to maintain
order, and soon the residents of nearby localities were allowed to spend their Sundays in peace.

A few years later Patrolman Cavagnaro moved to Apple
Island, and from that time on the island became a rendez-
vous for Charlestown residents. James J. Doherty built a
handsome cottage on the very foundations of Marsh's old
home, with a flagstaff in the front yard. Mr. Doherty's
brothers were quite often seen there spending their week-
ends with him. T. F. Harrington had a fine residence built
near the landing and called it the Hooker Camping Club of
Charlestown. William Hunter was well-known as a camper
here. But time brought many changes. In winter, gangs of
hoodlums went ashore and burned the summer cottages until
gradually all the houses disappeared.

The last couple to live at Apple Island was Milan R. Ober
and his wife, who moved there on July 15, 1932, building a
small residence. They spent an enjoyable summer at the
island, but during a gale in the first week in November the
house in which they had been living was lifted up into the
air and blown over the cliff to the beach. Luckily they were
both ashore at the time. The Obers did not rebuild.

When we walked across the ice to Apple Island on February 1, 1935, the cliff on the eastern side was breaking way
in huge slabs and slipping into the sea. It was a most impres-

sive sight, with great pieces of earth, thirty inches thick and sometimes fifteen feet square, lying diagonally against the cliff.

Apple Island was believed at one time a likely site for a fort, but the plans were never carried through. It was on February 25, 1826, that the War Department reported the island an ideal location for harbor defense work.

On June 29, 1935, it was announced that the "Suffolk Downs Associates," a group of citizens from East Boston, Chelsea, and Revere, desired to take over the island to erect suitable buildings there for recreational purposes.

In 1946 the island was flattened out to become part of Logan International Airport.

The Apple Island legend is a tragic one. Some ten years before Marsh landed there for the first time, it is said that a beautiful young girl, a descendant of one of the royal governors, was missed from home, and a few weeks later her lifeless body was recovered from the waters off Apple Island. Since a band of robbers was living on the island at that time, the young girl's sweetheart at once suspected that the men were the cause of his lady's death. Nothing was heard from him for weeks, until a friend finally disclosed that he had gone to the island and joined the robber band in order to find out the details of the girl's death.

One day a fisherman was sailing by the island, and as was usually the case, looked at the tall elm that stood at the top of the island to get his bearings. From the lower limb of the elm there hung a body! Knowing about the robber band, he did not dare go ashore, but on reaching Boston he notified the authorities, who dispatched armed men to the spot. When the body was cut down, it was found to be that of the young man who had tried to avenge his sweetheart's

Photo by Frederick G. S. Clow

Minot's Light

Photo by Frederick G. S. Clow

OPPOSITE: Corridor of dungeons, Fort Warren

Confederate prisoners, the *Tacomy* and *Atlanta* crews, at
Fort Warren, 1864

Boston Light

Vorth Prospect of the Light House

Boston Light, 1720

View of Castle Island from Dorchester Point, 1773

EW of *CASTLE WILLIAM* at Station D.

Bob Kennedy, the author (center), and Commander Kenneth Black at Nix's Mate

OPPOSITE BOTTOM: Governor's Island. Dungeon Keep at left, entrance to three-hundred-foot tunnel at right

Dungeon Keep on Governor's Island

Point Cottage, known as the Greek Temple, on Rainsford's Island. The building was dedicated in 1826.

OPPOSITE TOP: Gallop's Island, 1944

OPPOSITE BOTTOM: Fort Strong and lighthouse on Long Island

Photo by Dan Murphy

Photo by Frederick G. S. Clow

ABOVE: Closeup of Graves Light

OPPOSITE TOP: Deer Island Light, about 1889

OPPOSITE BOTTOM: Graves Light, 1970

Bug Light, about 1875

OPPOSITE: Surf breaking against the granite sides of America's most dangerously located lighthouse, Minot's Light

Barton S. Alexander, the builder of Minot's Light

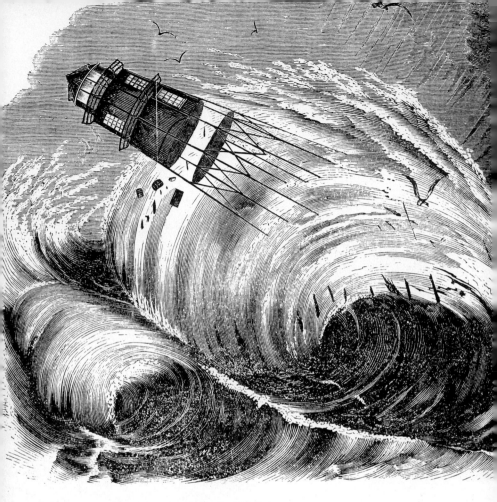

The destruction of Minot's Ledge Lighthouse

Minot's Ledge Lighthouse in winter, with salt spray frozen all the way to the top

Actress Julia Arthur's house on Middle Brewster, 1940

Seagulls rule the ruins of the razed house formerly owned by Julia Arthur on Calf Island.

Photo by Dan Murphy

death. There was not a robber left on the island, and they
never again returned to the scene of their double crime. The
ghosts of the two were said to be still walking up and down
the shores and around the great elm in 1900, but not for
many years have they been either seen or heard.

SNAKE ISLAND

Between Apple Island and the Winthrop shore lies an island
of three acres called Snake Island, the goal of scores of children as well as older folk from Winthrop. Here they play
pirates or dig in the sand, spending many happy hours in
the peaceful locality. Snake Island was so named because its
shape resembled a coiled serpent.

We know how heavily wooded all the islands were in
early colonial days, and possibly there were wild animals
at Snake Island at that time. At any rate, it is called Bare
Island on Fayrwether's Chart, which was printed about
1689. Just what Bare stood for will, in all probability, never
be known, but possibly the island was barren of trees. The
early history of the island is quite obscure, but we do know
that in 1720 Mehitabel Selby owned this little tract of land
off Winthrop's shore. Some time later it was purchased by
John Tenny, along with fifty-six acres at Pullen Point.

In the early days of the Revolutionary War, Snake Island
was mentioned in a resolve of the Committee of Safety for
May 14, 1775, as follows: "*Resolved*, as the opinion of this
Committee, that all the live-stock be taken from Noddle's
Island, Hog Island, Snake Island, and from that part of
Chelsea near the sea-coast." James Lloyd Homer speaks of
an unsuccessful treasure hunt at Snake Island around 1830.

Perhaps the treasure still awaits some romantic person who is willing to dig up the entire island to find the buried gold which has so far eluded all searchers.

The Treworgy brothers from Winthrop lived on Snake Island in 1900 in the cabin of the deserted steamer *United States*. They tended about 150 lobster traps around the Harbor. Although they did not stay on the property the year round, they came to the island about the first of March and left around the middle of November. One of the brothers was drowned from his boat off the island a few years later, and the other brother finally gave up the lobster business and left the island.

The island had passed into the possession of the Tewksburys and the Belchers and was sold for tax claims to Captain Samuel G. Irwin for twelve dollars. O. E. Lewis had purchased the land late in the nineteenth century from Captain Irwin; in 1912 the several squatters on the island were told that the three-dollar yearly fee they had been paying to stay on the Island would be raised to ten dollars. The shack on the south side of the island was the home of James Adams. The cabin occupied by Horton D. Fullerton was next in line, while the residence of Bill Carey, whose Portuguese name did not at all resemble his new American one, came next. The latter's hut boasted the only flagstaff on the island, from which the Stars and Stripes floated on the breeze Sundays and holidays. Next door was John Green, over whose door the sign "Welcome to Guests" somewhat surprised the casual visitor. Judson G. Fullerton lived nearest Winthrop's shore in a small shack. Another man by the name of Hunt made his home there at this time. Each man was in the lobster-trapping and clam-digging business.

The Winthrop Board of Health finally decreed against

the occupation of Snake Island, and gradually the inhabitants moved away to less deserted shores. It has been many years since a house has stood on Snake Island, and probably many more will pass before some venturesome person again dares to locate there.

8

RAINSFORD'S, GALLOP'S, AND LOVELL'S ISLANDS

RAINSFORD'S ISLAND

Owen Rowe, writing to John Winthrop during the winter of 1636, requested that "Mr. Ransford may be accommodated with lande for a farme." Thereupon the Puritan Government gave Elder Edward Rainsford a small island of eleven acres located between Peddock's and Long Islands, about a seven miles' sail from Boston. This island has for many years been called one of the Harbor's prettiest, but in its present ruinous state it is hardly attractive from the channel. West Head still contains many delightful nooks and coves, however, and the High Bluff on the eastern side is a well-known landmark. This bluff slopes away on the inside to form a flat area large enough for a baseball diamond. Between this land and West Head there is a narrow strip of beach, formerly wide enough for a road but now barely passable at high tide. When seen from the air, the island resembles an elongated animal.

Edward Rainsford, or Raynsford as the name was sometimes spelled, was the brother of Sir Richard Rainsford, Lord Chief Justice of the King's Bench. At the time of the Antinomian Controversy, the Puritans declared Rainsford a heretic and disarmed him. Elder Rainsford lived to a good old age and died on August 16, 1680. His widow, who survived him by eight years, is buried in King's Chapel graveyard.

In 1735 the shipowners of Boston were discussing the advisability of transferring the Quarantine Station from Spectacle Island to a more suitable location and considered Rainsford's Island with favor. The committee appointed to visit the island reported that it was a satisfactory location.

The hospital was moved here from Spectacle Island in 1737, but before this, the island seems to have been used either by the Indians or the colonists as a burial ground. An incident which occurred many years later confirms this idea. Dr. J. V. C. Smith, on the island in the spring of 1826, watched a lad setting up posts around some young trees. The boy drove his crowbar into one of the many sunken pits and found a human skull in a fairly good state of preservation. Smith believed that the sunken pits near the old fever hospital were ancient graves, but both history and tradition are silent concerning them. About this time a most unusual stone grave was discovered containing a skeleton with an iron sword hilt, possibly suggesting the burial place of that ancient Norseman, Thorwald.

Diarist Ezekial Price wrote on September 2, 1778, of his visit here with many prominent dignitaries to view the French fleet then in the Harbor.

Thomas Spear, the hero of the Lovers' Rock tragedy, became keeper of Rainsford's Island in 1796, holding the position until his death in 1812. He is buried in the cemetery here, near his son George, who succeeded Thomas Spear as keeper.

A frequent visitor to Rainsford's Island in 1819 was Rev. Frederick W. A. S. Brown, who lived at Deer Island during the summer and visited many of the islands around the harbor that year. Brown's impressions of Rainsford's Island follow:

> *To Rainsford's little pleasant isle,*
>   *Does precedence belong;*
> *Here kindness dwells and Hobart's smile*
>   *Your welcome would prolong.*
>
> *While Welch, the son of healing art,*
>   *Will due prescription give;*
> *And use each mean to soothe the heart*
>   *And make the suff'rer live.*
>
> *Here sprightly youth may exercise*
>   *Upon the bowling green;*
> *When no rude storms deform the skies,*
>   *And nature shines serene.*

The island in 1826 had many buildings which were torn down before the start of the present century, but we have a fairly good idea of how they looked. There was a large two-story dwelling house shaped like the letter L, a licensed tavern for the accommodation of those who arrived by sea. The keeper's family lived here and enjoyed the library of the tavern, which during the summer months contained newspapers and magazines from all over the United States. To the east of the dwelling house stood the smallpox hospital, while off by itself, on a rise in the ground, the fever hospital faced the west.

Since the object of quarantine laws is to prevent the introduction of contagious diseases from abroad, all foreign vessels had to anchor in President Road to await examination by the port physician in charge. When a ship arrived, the physician and island keeper went aboard, gave the master a red flag which was displayed from the masthead, and set about to examine both crew and cargo. A list of regulations that had to be complied with was left aboard the ship, and the physician fixed the time when the vessel was to be discharged, providing the regulations were obeyed. They included purification of all bedding, clothes, and cargo, pumping out the bilge water, and an accurate list of all persons on the ship. On passing all the requirements the master was given a certificate.

The Quarantine Station was moved from Rainsford's Island in 1849. Dr. Smith, who later became mayor of Boston, spent much of his time engraving historical facts and pert proverbs on rocks all over the island. He was not alone, however, for there are scores of other signatures and messages in many languages dating back to 1647. Perhaps the oldest signature is that of Raynsford, presumably written by the man himself. I have spent many days on the island trying to decipher the various inscriptions on both gravestones and rocks on the shore. On the southwestern bluff, between the fever hospital of 1832 and the graveyard, the following epitaph, now gone, was cut into a rock:

> *Nearby these gray rocks*
> *Enclos'd in a box*
> *Lies Hatter Cox*
> *Who died of smallpox.*

A few feet away one could read:

> *Stones tell tales.*
> *Time draws teeth.*
> *Search & see.*

On the southeastern shore of the West Head there is a flat, sloping rock formation, in which scores of inscriptions have been chiseled. I have copied most of them, but realizing the reader may not share my enthusiasm, I include only a few:

Dr. T. Welch was here 26 yrs.
Dr. J. V. C. Smith was appointed June 14, 1826
C. P. Tewksbury was appointed Island Keeper in July, 1841

Tewksbury met his death some years later when a bomb exploded at a Fourth of July celebration on Boston Common.

This century-old Latin advice should interest the scholar:

Specta mantum, non frontem hominis, nam,
Verumdecus, est, positum, in virtute.
Insula Rupes. A.D. 1835

Essentially the translation tells one to

Look to the character of the man,
Not his outward appearance;
For true worth lies in virtue.

On this ledge we also read that the island was purchased from the Indians for a pig and a pullet. Walking around toward the western part of the bluff, we find engraved the following advice to the drunkard, which, judging from what I have seen in the past few years on the island, has not been noticed by all of the visitors:

He who violates sobriety
Surely will never prosper.
Brandy is Death's first turnkey,
The tomb the tipler's early prison.

Every gravestone in the cemetery was moved to Long

Island some years ago. The earliest legible gravestone on the island reads as follows:

*M*ʳ. *Ithamer Ward*
1749

Another inscription which is often seen on gravestones of the period was on the stone of Nancy Smith, who died August 20, 1802:

Behold and see as you pass by,
As you are now, so once was I;
As I am now, so you must be
Prepare for death and follow me.

Then there was the stone of Lieutenant Horace Stockton White who died on board the brig *Henrico* in 1812. He was one of the two sons of Moses White of Rutland, Massachusetts, both of whom met untimely deaths. His brother Francis was killed by Lieutenant William Finch in a duel at Noddle's Island in 1817.

Richard Henry Dana, in 1836, sailed by Hospital Island in the *Alert* on his way back from California, having left San Diego 135 days before. Dana looked down from the royal yard of his ship, seeing the "island, with its hospital buildings, nice graveled walks, and green plats."

After the Quarantine Station was changed to Deer Island in 1847, the state took over Rainsford's Island and established the Massachusetts almshouse there. When the Commonwealth changed its plans in 1866, Boston bought the island for $40,000, making it the site for the city almshouse. It was during this period that the Civil War veterans lived here. In 1882 they were removed to the Soldiers Home on Powder Horn Hill, Chelsea.

When the city of Boston purchased Long Island in 1882, the male paupers were taken across to Long Island from

Rainsford's Island, and the female inmates from Austin Farm took their place. In 1895 the women at Rainsford's were also transferred to Long Island.

Before 1895, boys committed for misdemeanors were sent to Deer Island for discipline and lived there with the men and women prisoners. The boys were transferred to Rainsford's Island in 1895. At three different times between 1912 and 1918 boys tried to escape. On June 15, 1912, George Kelly, aged fourteen, and twelve-year-old Michael Bongrene set out from their prison home on the island in a canoe. They landed at Moon Head but were captured a short time later by the Quincy police.

The following year, at 10:15 P.M. on July 7, Arthur Allen, Frederick McGinley, and John Scully, all thirteen years old, attempted a getaway. Throwing off their night clothes, they plunged into the water and started to swim to Joe's Rock about four hundred yards away. A cry for help was heard by the night watchman, but all he discovered were the night clothes on the beach. The next morning John Scully was found at the house on Joe's Rock, or Quarantine Ledge, but the other two boys could not be located. On the seventeenth of July the body of Fred McGinley was taken from the water off Winthrop by a sailor aboard the *Bumpus*, a War Department boat. Arthur Allen's body was found a week later near Graves Light.

The great escape came on February 21, 1918, when the Harbor was frozen solid around the island. Seven boys ran over the ice to freedom that morning, and six more followed them later in the day. As it was the first time in a quarter century that the Harbor had been frozen over as far as Rainsford's Island, the boys made the best of this opportunity. Their freedom was short-lived as one by one they were captured and brought back.

The same month the "Greek Temple," which had been

the subject of a Robert Salmon painting, burned to the ground. The smaller boys located there had to be crowded in with the older children. Conditions became so unfavorable at the school that the authorities agreed to give up the school, which at this time had 126 boys. Commissioner O'Brien said that the boys would be transferred to Westboro and Shirley, but planned a gradual change, as the schools in those towns were crowded. The boys were removed from the island one by one, and no more commitments were allowed. On the last day of 1920 the school closed for good.

For many years Portuguese Joe's house withstood the elements on Quarantine Rocks off Rainsford's Island. Built on stilts, it served as lobster headquarters around the Harbor for two generations. Portuguese Joe was noted for the fact that occasionally the lobsters he sold were not quite of legal length. Finally he made enough money for his declining years and returned to the Cape Verde Islands, where he was born.

On several occasions in 1935, '36, and '37, our History Club of the Winthrop High School went ashore and explored the three-story building. Portuguese Joe's "house on the rocks" was entirely destroyed by fire in 1938 and only an iron rod or two remained to identify this once popular Boston Harbor location.

In the spring of the year 1935 the stable on the island was gutted. Now, for the first time in almost three hundred years, Rainsford's Island is without a building worthy of the name.

GALLOP'S ISLAND

About a quarter-mile to the southwest of Lovell's Island and a mile to the northeast of Rainsford's Island lies Gallop's Island, formerly the location of the Quarantine Station for Boston. On December 30, 1916, the Government paid $150,000 for the island which in 1649, according to the will of John Gallop, was worth the equivalent of $75. Captain Gallop was mentioned frequently in early maritime accounts of Boston Harbor; his spectacular encounter with the Indians who had scalped his friend John Oldham will always remain an epic in the history of New England.

John Gallop, with his two little boys and a friend, were sailing off the coast of Block Island when they saw a small pinnace which they thought looked familiar. It was the boat of John Oldham, so they drew alongside. Finding the deck occupied by fifteen Indians, they knew something was wrong. In the terrific encounter which followed, eleven of the Indians were killed, and when one surrendered, Gallop bound and threw him into the water. The remaining Indians fled below deck and were made prisoners. Now in possession of the boat, Gallop started to look for his friend Oldham. He found the body under an old seine, "stark naked, his head cleft to the brains, and his hands and legs cut as if they had been cutting them off, and yet warm." Gallop and his crew lowered John Oldham's body into the sea, and sorrowfully sailed back to Boston Harbor. John Gallop died around 1649; his aforementioned will can still be seen in the Suffolk Files at the Boston Court House.

The shape of this island has been likened by Shurtleff to that of a leg of mutton, with the shank pointing easterly across the Narrows to Bug Light. The fixed beacon that flashes its warning a few score feet from Beachy Point at Gallop's Island is known as Peggy's Point, where Peggy waited in vain for her missing lover, who had been drowned at sea.

Lemuel Brackett of Quincy paid $1,630 for the old In-

dian fighter's former residence. At this time Peter Newcomb, the tenant of the island, made plans to purchase it for
himself. These plans finally materialized on July 1, 1819,
when Brackett sold his tenant the island for $1,815. An old
fort was still in existence at the time of this sale. Eight years
later $2,429.51 was appropriated to cut down the cliff so as
to eliminate too commanding a view on the future Fort
Warren. So much of the soil from the cliffs was washing
away at this time that Dr. J. V. C. Smith believed that the
island would disappear before 1860. Peter Newcomb, who
had a fine farm on Gallop's Island, died on April 22, 1833,
and his passing was regretted by his island neighbors. His
wife Margaret stayed on at the island, opening an eating
establishment there a few years later. Spending a week at
Newcomb's Island soon became the custom of many Bostonians, and Mrs. Newcomb's cooking came to have a very
enviable reputation around the city. When Mrs. Newcomb
died, her son Charles sold the property to the city of Boston,
receiving $6,500. Joe Snow purchased Mrs. Newcomb's
boarding house about 1855, and as Snow's Island it became
known as the scene of many lively chowders and clam
bakes. His daughter Peggy has Peggy's Point Light off the
Island named in her memory.

Boston loaned the island to the Government during the
Civil War, and hundreds of soldiers were soon encamped
on the slopes of Peter Newcomb's old farm.

With the coming of peace and the threatened infection
from disease, the deserted barracks at Gallop's Island were
turned over to the city. On June 1, 1866, the Quarantine
Station for Boston Harbor was moved from Deer Island to
Gallop's Island. The first twenty years of quarantine there
saw an annual average of fifty patients, and in the hillside
cemetery there are 248 graves of those who failed to recover

from their sickness, in addition to twelve who died during the Civil War.

In June 1912, Councilor Earnest E. Smith of Boston said that Boston was the only great port on the Atlantic Coast which paid for the regulation of quarantine, which in 1911 cost $22,700. Smith recommended that the Government be asked to take over Gallop's Island. After various negotiations lasting until December 1916, Assistant District-Attorney Hatton gave the city of Boston a check for $150,000, and the United States assumed control of Boston Harbor quarantine.

A year later, when America entered the First World War, the German sailors who were on the interned ships in Boston were taken down to the island. These sailors had ruined the engines of their German ships before abandoning them, and were at Gallop's Island for the duration of the war as prisoners.

The island's most active period was during the Second World War when the Maritime Training School was established here.

After graduation the hundreds of officers who were to sail all over the world had a very impressive ritual as they left the island, in most cases forever. In a little circle just off the head of the pier a monument had been erected showing a ship sinking to the bottom of the ocean. The plot around the monument was always kept dug up. As the men came down the long walk and then ended their descent of the cement staircase, they would march at attention toward the statue of the sinking ship. In the tightly clenched left hand of each man was a bundle of pennies, and each man in turn would approach to within a few feet of the monument. Then, snapping into a salute with his right hand, the officer would toss the pennies into the fresh soil at the base of the monument, after which he would complete his salute, walk around the monument and onto the pier, where he would board the boat for Boston.

In the years immediately following the war I watched visitors to the island as they searched in the loam for the pennies thrown by the men of yesterday. When the island was given up by the Government shortly after the war, the monument was moved to the Fenway in sight of the Museum of Fine Arts, where I visited it recently.

During one of my visits to Gallop's during the war I was invited to give a lecture on the Harbor and then stay overnight. In the middle of the night the old pest house was consumed by flames. At the height of the blaze the men awakened me so that I could photograph in color the burning building. I made several hundred feet of film, but because of the war was not allowed to take it off the island. I was assured that within a few weeks it would be censored and delivered to me. I am still awaiting the film.

Another memory of my wartime visits to Gallop's Island is of the giant gymnasium building. We often played basketball in pick-up teams against the officers. Afterward we would go down one flight and visit the cafeteria, where they made us the most delightful chocolate frappes for only a dime.

Gallop's Island has undergone many ups and down since the days of the Government Quarantine Station there. Today, unless there is a serious condition aboard a craft entering Boston Harbor, all clerical work can be done by radio, thus eliminating for all practical purposes the older type of quarantine station. The island is now deserted.

The famous pirate "Long Ben" Avery buried his money at Point Shirley, where it was later dug up, but his diamonds, including the mate to the famous Orloff diamond, are yet to be found where Avery buried them—at Gallop's Island, centuries ago. Perhaps they will still be discovered.

LOVELL'S ISLAND

"Lovell's Island is graunted to Charlestowne provided they imploy it for fishing by their own townesmen, or hinder not others."

This significant entry on the twenty-eighth of October, 1636, is the first mention we have of the island probably named after William Lovell of Dorchester. In 1648 Charlestown was again given permission to use the island, "pvided that halfe of the timber & fire wood shall belonge to the garrison at the Castle." Nantasket strenuously objected to Charlestown's owning the Island, but in vain. James Brown was allowed to live there at this time if he would set up a "stage" and follow the fishing trade. The first recorded disaster occurred in 1645, when a ketch from the inner Harbor pulled her moorings and smashed to pieces on the shores of Lovell's Island. George Worthylake, the first keeper of Boston Light, moved here about 1700 from George's Island.

Lovell's Island is located about a mile and a half to the southeast of Deer Island and is approximately three quarters of a mile long and one third of a mile wide. Many of its acres washed away before a seawall was erected to protect the island. It is separated from Gallop's Island by the Narrows.

About a century and a half ago there was a large tree standing on the southern point of Lovell's Island which was used as a marker by the mariners coming up the Harbor. Because of a blinding snowstorm in 1767, the captain of a brig was unable to see the marker and lost his bearings. The ship crashed on the beach at Lovell's Island, the vessel luckily holding together until the next morning when the sea subsided enough to allow the passengers to reach the shore. A little girl was lowered over the side of the ship by a rope. This little girl, Susanna Haswell, grew up to become a very versatile women, well-known as author, actress, and school-teacher; such a combination today would indeed be unusual. Later in life she married and became Mrs. Rowson. Her novel, *Rebecca*, describes the shipwreck on lonely Lovell's Island.

In 1782 the great French fleet of Admiral Vaubaird sailed into Boston Harbor. A Boston pilot, David Darling, was unfortunate enough to wreck the great *Magnifique*, a man-of-war of seventy-four guns, on a bar leading from the West Head of Lovell's Island. Badly damaged, she filled and sank in deep water right off the inner shore. Whether the day was stormy or the pilot alone was at fault probably will never be known, but David Darling lost his job.

It was a sad day for the new republic when Darling's piloting carried the vessel to her doom, for America felt obliged to give France as compensation her own seventy-four gun ship then nearing completion at Portsmouth, New Hampshire. The boat was launched on November 5, 1782, but when John Paul Jones found that he was not to command the new battleship, he resigned from the service, and America lost the man who was perhaps her greatest naval hero. Thus we have the carelessness of a young Boston pilot contributing to the final chapter in the career of a great commander. David Darling, the unfortunate pilot, obtained a position as sexton of the Old North Church, succeeding Robert Newman. Shurtleff tells us that the children of the

North End bothered the poor man by writing in chalk on
the door of the church:

> *Don't you run this ship ashore*
> *As you did the seventy-four.*

David Darling was buried in the Copp's Hill cemetery
on September 10, 1820, and the skeleton of the *Magnifique*, buried under tons of sand, was quite forgotten by the
average Bostonian. Our "Shade of Alden," James Lloyd
Homer, was sailing up the Narrows a quarter of a century
later, and as he looked over at Lovell's Island an old man
stepped up to him and mentioned the story of the *Magnifique*. The elderly gentleman told Homer he well remembered the day the *Magnifique* went down and pointed out
the exact spot of the wreck. The currents of the Narrows
had created a bar over the hulk in the sixty-three years that
had passed since the man-of-war went down, and possibly
Homer's mention of the incident caused some of the treasure seekers to make an attempt for the gold which was lost
with the ship.

Attempts had already been made around 1840 to recover
the treasure from the *Magnifique*, but they had failed.
Again in July 1859, excavations were made, but all that the
searchers could find were some beautiful pieces of wood
from the hull of the ship. During 1868 and 1869 more tim-
bers were uncovered, but, since nothing of intrinsic value
was found, it was decided to abandon further attempts.
When Shurtleff visited the island, he found that the spot
where the *Magnifique* had gone down was not covered by
water even at high tide, thus showing how the contour of
Lovell's Island had changed since the 1782 wreck.

Continuing with the story of the *Magnifique*, we move
to the twentieth century. On a cool spring morning fifty

years ago, Keeper Charles H. Jennings was industriously digging near his house on the island when suddenly his spade struck an object that resembled a coin. Jennings stooped and picked it up. He continued his excavations until he had unearthed many of the round, flat disks. Taking them into his house, he scrubbed and dug the deposit away from one of the objects, and there was revealed a gold coin, worth by its size and weight about $29. The other coins yielded under the rubbing and scrapping to reveal that they, too, were valuable silver and gold pieces of long ago.

Jennings, however, was about to leave the island on his annual vacation, and when the assistant arrived at the lighthouse station, Jennings told him the interesting news. He noticed that the assistant seemed quite attentive to his account of how he found the gold and silver, but Jennings promptly forgot all about the incident as he boarded the afternoon boat for the mainland.

When Jennings returned from his vacation on the mainland, the assistant left the island as soon as possible with all his baggage. Walking up to his house, Jennings went around to the spot where he had dug up the coins, and there was a deep, yawning hole. A few months later the assistant retired from the Lighthouse Service and lived in comfort for the rest of his life. The reader may draw his own conclusions.

Four years after the wreck of the *Magnifique* the most tragic incident in the history of Lovell's Island took place. On the fourth of December, 1786, a packet from Maine, under Captain Atkins, crashed on the beach at the eastern side of the island. A bitter snow storm was sweeping up the coast. All of the passengers and crew were successful in reaching the shore, but they could find no shelter anywhere on the island. At the top of the hill was a large rock which gave them some protection against the fierce blizzard which was raging. There the people, thirteen in number, huddled in their wet clothing as the thermometer went lower and lower.

With the coming of dawn, a fisherman on a neighboring island, Thomas Spear by name, noticed the wreck and crossed over. He saw the group crouched together in the shelter of the rock and went up the hill to investigate, finding all of the party apparently frozen to death. Among the group were two young people, Miss Sylvia Knapp and a young man whose name has been forgotten, who had been on their way to Boston to purchase furniture for their home-to-be. The two lovers were found locked in each other's arms.

Although the usual story told for almost a century and a half had been that all were frozen to death, the *New England Courant* for that period will reveal the fact that one man survived the terrible ordeal and lived for almost a fortnight afterward. He was Theodore Kingsley of Wrentham, Massachusetts. Thomas Spear brought him up to town as soon as possible, but he was so badly frozen that after lingering for many days, he grew worse and died. The story of the tragedy has been told by the Reverend Brown, and a few verses describing the incident follow:

> *The tempest hid the cheering Light,*
> * So thickly flew the snow;*
> *Alas, what horror fill'd the night,*
> * With bitter, piercing woe.*
>
> *At length they gained the sea-beat strand,*
> * And rescued from the waves;*
> *On Lovell's Island only land,*
> * To find more decent graves.*

Among the rest, a youthful pair,
Who from their early youth;
Had felt of love an equal share,
Adorn'd with equal truth,

Lay prostrate mid the dire alarms,
Had calm resign'd their breath;
Fast lock'd within each other's arms,
Together sunk to death.

A rabbit run on Lovell's Island supplied the markets of Boston for many years, and quite a few of the little pets of the boys and girls in the capital city came from this island down the Harbor.

In 1843 when the city petitioned for a seawall to be erected around Lovell's Island, the Government appropriated $15,000 for the preservation of William Lovell's old home. Sylvanus Thayer, Colonel of the United States Engineers, was in charge of the construction of the seawall at this time. He also erected stone jetties at the island six years later. Thus this master builder of forts has also left his mark at Lovell's Island.

In 1874 the Government established the Lighthouse Buoy Station at Lovell's Island. On the wharf were to be seen duplicates of many of the giant buoys located around the Harbor, ready for instant service whenever the occasion demanded. A track formerly ran from the wharf to the northern end of the island, which is called Ram's Head.

The War Department established Fort Standish on Lovell's Island soon after 1900, notifying the Lighthouse Department to look elsewhere. In 1902 the twin range lights were erected near Ram's Head and when the foundation for the lower light was being dug the skeleton of a man was found far under the surface. Whether or not the bones guarded some pirate's treasure has not as yet been discovered. The remains had been petrified.

A short time before midnight on October 10, 1933, the *City of Montgomery*, under Captain B. H. Garfield, failed to make the turn at Nix's Mate for the Narrows, and stuck fast against the bar at Lovell's Island. The force of the ship drove her high and she was on the rocky ledge so near the high water mark that at low tide Keeper Jennings of the range lights was able to walk right out to the ship. Luckily, no serious storm occurred while the ship was on the bar, and shortly after 11:15 P.M. on October 12, she was pulled off by the combined efforts of several tugs.

In many respects Lovell's Island was the Island of Romance. The two lighthouses, Lover's Rock, the treasure, the pirate's skeleton, and last but not least, the mysterious underground passageway which shoots off under the Harbor made up an unusual combination for one small island of sixty-two acres.

If any adventurous readers care to make the trip down the tunnel, don the oldest clothes you have. The location is easily found to the left of the steps leading up to the top of the hill. Opening the old studded door, we flash our lights into the darkness of the passageway to find that the arched tunnel takes a sharp turn to the right. Stumbling over mouldy journals and decayed newspapers, we walk for some time before coming to the next turn, where a shelf is built into the wall, looking as if it were made for a telephone. We again turn to the right, and continue down the passageway. Some twenty feet beyond, the corridor opens into a large, arched room having a rectangular hole in the middle of the floor. Anyone who did not bring a flashlight is surely in danger here.

Turning our light down into the opening, we see that the

hole is about five feet in depth; we jump down and find another surprise. The wall of the pit farthest away from the tunnel has an opening, and when we flash our light down we find another passageway which seems to be endless. At this point in our adventure quite a few of those who had declared their bravery in the sunlight decide they have had enough excitement for the time being and, telling us they will wait outside, beat a hasty retreat.

The only way we can travel through this new opening is on our hands and knees, as it is no higher than the space under the average office table. Crawling down this tunnel, we find we are gradually getting lower and lower. The end is reached at a point where the top of the passageway has caved in. Here we join the elect by scraping our names on the damp walls before starting on the long journey back to the sunlight. No one now on the island knows the history of this tunnel which once led out under the Harbor.

Perhaps the old tunnel was originally connected with the mysterious fort which is indicated as having been at Lovell's Island in 1700, although not a bit of evidence has ever been found concerning this strange four-bastioned fortification. The chart that shows this old fort was published in 1705, at London. Possibly the chart designers made a mistake, but if they did a good story is spoiled.

When the Second World War seemed certain around the year 1940, the island began to bustle with excitement. The place that once saw the landing of the pirates of Thomas Pound, later the establishment of two lighthouses, and still later the establishment of the buoy station, now began its most active period. Soon a score of half-tents were constructed there and later regulation barracks, so that within a relatively short time hundreds and hundreds of soldiers were living at the fort.

I recall my visit there when I lectured to the men about buried treasure, ghosts, and the pirates, and later photographed all available soldiers in one group.

The paper on the island was known as the *Sand Spit Sentinel.*

As the years went by the two lighthouses were torn down, the barracks disappeared one by one, and the fairly satisfactory pier was burned.

The Metropolitan District Commission has now erected a new pier, and I certainly hope that visitors will be allowed to go ashore on this island.

The S.O.S. or Save Our Shores group has carried out many projects here and on other islands in an effort to beautify Boston Bay.

9

NODDLE'S AND HOG ISLANDS

Both Noddle's Island and Hog Island, today known as East Boston, are now so much a part of the mainland, that their insular background is not realized by many.

Three hundred and forty-two years ago, in January 1629, John Gorges conveyed to Sir William Brereton, among other parcels of land, two islands that are today known as East Boston and Orient Heights. They were then called Brereton's Island for William Brereton, and Susanna Island for his daughter. We read in the Massachusetts Archives that Brereton sent over a small group of people to settle on his grants, but there is no proof that he personally visited either the island which bore his name or the mainland. Probably his battles in England took so much of his time that he was not able to journey to the New World. A contemporary, John Vicars, tells us that Brereton was "blessed by God with many memorable and famous Victories over his Countrie's enemies, notably beating that Arch Malignant enemy of those parts, Sir Thomas Ashton."

NODDLE'S ISLAND

Brereton's rights to this property were denied him in February 1629. William Noddle comes into this account of East Boston three hundred years ago. We will never know exactly when Noddle came to the island which was to bear his name, but he was probably living there when it was owned by Brereton. Noddle, who is among the list of freemen included in the 1631 Colony Records, was drowned in the ocean the following summer while carrying wood in his canoe. This original "Noddle-Islander" probably died without children, for we can find no further mention of the name Noddle in the early history of the settlement.

Noddle's Island, named for William Noddle, was included in 1631 with the islands appropriated for public uses, but the sole privilege of catching the waterfowl and pigeons there was given to Jobe Perkins. The island at this time, with its hundreds of birds, was surely a "happy hunting ground" for the alert Perkins. Samuel Maverick, who was living in the vicinity when the Puritans came into Boston Harbor, was quick to realize this fact, and saw to it that he was given the permit for 1633. Maverick was allowed by the Puritans to stay on Noddle's Island provided he made an annual payment of "either a fat wether, a fat hog, or 40s in money." The great John Winthrop visited Maverick at his humble home in June 1630. Prince's well-known chronology of that year tells us that "on this island, with the help of Mr. David Thompson [of Thompson's Island], he had built a small fort with four great guns to protect him from the Indians."

A traveler from England named John Josselyn went ashore at Noddle's Island. That afternon Josselyn went for a walk in the woods, following a path through the trees. He came upon what he believed to be a large pineapple plated with scales, and took hold of the object. "No sooner had I touched it," he tells us, "but hundreds of Wasps were about me." Stung repeatedly, his face was so swollen by the time he returned to the house that Maverick could only recognize him by his clothes.

Maverick moved to New York and took up residence at the house given him "in the Broadway" by the Duke of York.

On June 24, 1711, Boston saw a great flotilla sail into the Harbor. Its sixty-one ships constituted a larger fleet than Nelson had at the Battle of the Nile. Leaving their sick at George's Island, the officers sent the men to Noddle's Island. Scores of tents were soon scattered about the former residence of Samuel Maverick, and headquarters were established near the present location of Belmont Square. Ever since, the slope on which they camped has been known as Camp Hill. Two great reviews were staged by these picked regiments of Marlborough's finest.

Donald McKay's famous clipper ships were of course built at the East Boston shipyards. The *Flying Cloud*'s great 89-day record to San Francisco still stands. *The Sovereign of the Seas* also made a wonderful run of 430 miles in 24 hours. Across the Harbor on Castle Island now stands the McKay memorial.

Perhaps the gentleman best able to give us a picture of East Boston almost a century ago was George Frederick Benner. His account of school attendance at Noddle's Island should interest the present generation:

"On Monmouth Street, above Marion, a two and a half story house had been turned into a school with two rooms, Mrs. Buffum downstairs and Miss (Polly) Crafts upstairs.

When a child was punished, Miss Crafts called the culprit, told him to put out his tongue, on which she put a drop or two of a fiery mixture as a punishment. At that time, opposite the fire-station from Eutaw to Trenton Streets, was a vegetable garden that extended halfway to Meridian Street, and seemed to be common property, for we used to climb the fence and take white turnips."

Mr. Benner tells us of the old horse cars:

"The car would stop for passengers along the line—no white posts then—they were small cars which ran to and over the ferry. In winter straw was put on the car floors which soon became a filthy mess. Any coin dropped was lost." Swimming was a popular sport and Benner tells us that each boy could swim, having been taught by the very effective method of being thrown into the water by the older boys. The boys swam at the site of Donald McKay's shipyard, later occupied by the Tim Manson Lumberyard.

The days of George Benner have gone forever. East Boston is regaining its former importance by turning to the air. The magnificent East Boston Airport, which stretches its fingers far out over what was formerly Noddle's Island Flats, is a challenge to the rest of the country, and it is by air transportation that Boston may be able to win back some of the forgotten glory of the days when McKay, the Nova Scotia shipbuilder, dominated the shipping industry of the world.

HOG OR SUSANNA ISLAND

Susanna Island, joined quite firmly not only to Noddle's Island but to the mainland as well, is known at the present time as Orient Heights. Mention of Susanna or Hog Island, as it later became known, is only occasional, but I have managed to obtain a few facts about the present home of the great Suffolk Downs racing establishment.

Probably the best known of all the owners of Hog or Susanna Island was Samuel Sewall. We can trace his visits thence by reading his voluminous diary. Sewall took possession of Hog Island on May 2, 1687, performing an elaborate ceremony with two columns of witnesses watching the proceedings. Sewall tells us his friends "watched my taking Livery and seised of the Lland by Turf and Twigg and the House." On July first he returned to Hog Island and made plans for building a pier or "Causey to land handsomly." At this time there were some fine cherry trees growing at Orient Heights, for Sewall brought home a basket filled with the fruit. By 1712 there were evidently many trees growing on Hog Island, for Sewall brought back to Boston three cords of wood in one afternoon.

John Breed, who bought the island in 1813, built a wonderful stone mansion on the southern slopes of Hog Island Hill. It was two hundred feet long and one story in height; its beautiful garden was a pleasure to behold. Breed died suddenly in 1846, and when his relatives visited the island they found $5,000 in silver stored in a cave on the hillside. Two great horse pistols, which, according to legend, never left his side, were found near his body. His will gave most of the property to his brother Richard, then living in England.

A century ago, in excavating for the radial highway which passes over Breed's Hill, the shovel brought up John Breed's old pump log. Sections of the long timber have been preserved in the Orient Heights Library and the Deane Winthrop House for the sight of future generations.

10

PEDDOCK'S ISLAND AND HINGHAM BAY

A mile south of Fort Warren and a quarter mile from Windmill Point in Hull lies Peddock's Island, which has more shore line than any other island in the Harbor. East Head is the present site of Fort Andrews, while the rest of the island is occupied by the various summer and winter residents. West Head faces Hough's Neck, and is a little more than half a mile from the Nut Island Pumping Station.

The earliest incident to be connected with Peddock's Island occurred some years before the Pilgrims landed at Plymouth. A French trading vessel was riding anchor off the shores of the island when the Indians massacred all the men except five whom they saved to exhibit around to the various tribes of Massachusetts. Years later, Morton of Merry Mount interviewed one of the Indians who had murdered the Frenchmen, and the Indian explained how the massacre took place:

"I said to the Sachem, 'I will tell you how you shall have all for nothing. Bring all our Canows and all our Beaver & a great many men, but no bow nor Arrow Clubs, nor

Hachits, but knives under your scins yt About our Lines. Throw vp much Beaver vpon thayr Deck; sell it very Cheep & when I giue the word, thrust yor knives in the French mens Bellys.' Thus we killed ym all. But Monesar Ffinch, Master of thayr ship, being wounded Leped into Ye hold. We bid him com vp, but he would not. Then we cutt thayr Cable & ye Ship went Ashore & lay upon her sid & slept ther. Ffinch cam vp & we killed him. Then our Sachem devided thayr goods and ffiered theyr Ship & It maed a very greaat fier."

Although the account does not mention the men spared, Stark tells us that when a Captain Dermer was cruising around Cape Cod early in the seventeenth century, he found two of the Frenchmen still alive and took them away after paying the ransom. Captain Dermer asked the Indians why they had killed the other Frenchmen. The Indians were not able to give a satisfactory answer, and the Englishman said that the Gods would be angry with them. A short time afterward the entire section was visited by a terrible plague, probably smallpox, and the redmen died by the hundreds. A reminder of this fatal sickness is still to be found at Nantasket, where Skull Head was so named because of the great number of unburied skeletons which the English settlers found at this spot.

The first mention of Peddock's Island by the Puritans is found in the records for September 3, 1634, when "Peddocks Ileland is graunted to the inhabitants of Charlton to enjoy to them and their heires, for the space of one & twenty yeares for the yearely rent of twenty shillings pvided that if there be a plantacon in the meane time setled by the Court att then ther pre^{nt} graunt to be voyde." As Nantasket was settled in 1641, Peddock's Island became a part of its territory. Leonard Peddock was the man for whom the island was named, but whether or not he ever lived on the island is not known. We find the following item in the New England Council's records for November 19, 1622: "It is ordered that a letter be written from the Counsell to Mr. Weston, to Leonard Peddock."

Peddock's Island was divided into lots of four acres each, to be given to those owning a two-acre section across the Gut at Hull. About the year 1700, certain family names appear quite frequently in the Suffolk Deeds; the Chamberlains and Lorings are among those prominently mentioned. The reader may realize the peculiar system of allotting the land by reading the following items, picked at random from the records in the Suffolk Registry of Deeds:

Dec. 6, 1722—Benjamin Loring et al to Thomas Jones . . . On Pettocks Island 2 acres.

April 1, 1754—John Loring, Jr. . . . . On Petix Island. The Sea 3 pcs. about 3 1/4 acres 16 acres 9 1/2 acres.

1795 April 14—Daniel Loring to John Haskins Jr. . . . . Hull at Padox Island on the Sea 4 a.

As the above would indicate, the recorders were consistently inconsistent in their spelling of Leonard Peddock's island. I have found twelve other combinations of letters for this same name.

During the Revolution Peddock's Island, together with so many others, was raided by the Continental troops for the sheep and cattle, five hundred sheep and thirty cattle being safely carried to the mainland. August 1776 saw many hundreds of colonial militia organizations encamped at Peddock's Island ready to meet any effort of the British fleet to return to Boston Harbor. Since the English did not return, the soldiers later withdrew to the mainland for other duties. Two years later Count D'Estaing's battered French fleet took refuge in Boston Harbor, many of the marines landing on Peddock's Island. The legend has come down that these French marines constructed fortifications on East Head, and there is some authority for that belief. Chevalier mentions another island besides George's Island on which fortifications were erected in 1778, and Peddock's, as anyone who has seen it would readily agree, was the logical site. In 1882 Sweetser mentioned that the "faint remains of the old entrenchments are still pointed out."

In 1817 there were three farmhouses on Peddock's Island, all located near the present site of the Fort Andrews wharf. They were probably the same houses of which a photograph was made in 1878. The Cleverly family occupied the residences a greater part of the century, both father and son being pilots for Nantasket and Hingham Bay.

In 1844 the whole island, with the exception of Middle Hill and Prince's Head, was owned by Thomas Jones, the grandfather of Eliza A. J. H. Andrew, who was the wife of Governor Andrew of Massachusetts. In 1860 Miss Sally Jones was the owner of the property, but on her death it passed to Mrs. Andrew. Governor Andrew died, and in 1897 his widow gave the Government a quit-claim for the eighty-eight acres needed for fortifications. Under General Order Number 43, April 4, 1900, the post became officially known as Fort Andrews in honor of General Leonard Andrews, a Civil War hero. For many years Bostonians believed it had been named in honor of Governor Andrew, but of course they were in error.

Colonel S. C. Vestal was commander of the first garrison at Fort Andrews in May 1904. Under him were Lieutenant James E. Wyke and Post Surgeon Luke B. Peck. Colonel Vestal spent considerable time in setting down various historical and topographical points concerning the island, and his fine work has become a permanent part of the War Department records.

Later on, during the fall of 1908, managers of the resorts on the island, the Y. O. West End House, and the Island Inn, were under suspicion for conducting gambling houses and similar establishments. As a result, on July 29, 1909, Chief of Police Reynolds of Hull arrested John Irwin, proprietor of the Island Inn. W. L. Drake, who ran the other resort, was not on the island when the police landed. In the case which developed it was brought out that so-called Chinese picnics were the primary factor in bringing the action. A rather amusing part of the procedure was that at the time of his arrest John Irwin was Chief of Police at Peddock's Island. Irwin was let off with a slight fine, but activities at the island were thereafter conducted in a more orderly fashion.

During the First World War there were possibly two thousand troops quartered at one time at Peddock's Island, mostly belonging to the original 55th Regiment and its subsequent replacements. In 1940, tucked away on the lee side of East Head, facing Hough's Neck and Quincy, was a row of houses where retired non-commissioned officers resided. If we walked from Sergeant Clark's residence through the pine grove on the north side of the Head, we could go down the path and reach the attractive house of Sergeant Frederick Perry, who retired in 1932. He lived here with his wife Lillian, and daughter Mary Louise, and had a fine motor boat which took him to the mainland. In the next house lived Alex Bies, who retired in 1918. He was married, having a daughter and two sons. The next residence was the home of former Sergeant Quinn, who visited the island every weekend. Sergeant Sam Perry came here with Captain S. C. Vestal in 1904, and occupied the southernmost house of the row.

Two tragic events were remembered by former Sergeant Perry. In the summer of 1906 two soldiers were drowned

while returning to George's Island from Peddock's when
the rowboat they were in tipped over passing through Hull
Gut. The men were Private Dan Doherty, former Lynn
baseball player of the New England League, and another
soldier, Private Crowley. Private Hunt was also with them
at the time, but stayed with the boat and was picked up by
the *De Hart*, the commanding officer's boat. Doherty was
drowned under the boat; Crowley swam to Peddock's
Island to summon aid. He then tried to swim back to the
boat to help Hunt but evidently tired and drowned. In 1934
another tragedy took place when a retired revenue service
man, Hayden by name, died from exposure on the island,
alone and unable to ask for help. When his body was discovered, the Bay was frozen over, and the Coast Guardsmen
from Point Allerton Station made the difficult trip over the
ice to bring his remains to Nantasket.

I recall meeting middle-aged Manuel Silva and his son
Joseph in 1935 in their home on the western slope of the
central hill. Manuel first lived at Long Island, where he
settled in 1893. Two years later, he and many others were
requested to leave Long Island when the city decided to put
off all squatters. Coming to Peddock's Island, he built a
house on East Head and lived there until the Government
bought the land for Fort Andrews. He then moved to Central Hill, building the house in which he was living when I
visited him. Joseph Silva well remembered the night of the
Portland storm and the Christmas storm of 1909.

He also remembered, about the year 1890, seeing Indians
on the lowland. He watched them hunt seals off the island
for the two-dollar bounty. What a far cry from the Indians
who scalped the Frenchmen over three centuries before, to
these civilized red men who wore the dress of the white
man!

Other people who had long made Peddock's Island their

home were John Pinto, Joseph Alberts, A. P. Silva, Manuel Ferrara, Walter Enos, and Mrs. Gram, who formerly ran a delightful tea room on the island. Bernard Silva conducted a summertime store there. Joseph Silva said that the West End House was burned years ago; the house erected in its place on West Bluff was burned in 1935. Irwin's Island Inn disappeared long ago, and many new cottages have made their appearance, until Central Hill is now a thriving summer colony.

Let us walk along the bar to Prince's Head, the southeast extremity of Peddock's Island, which was named for Job Prince, a seventeenth-century mariner. It was once the site of the great target at which Norman Wiard's guns were fired from Nut Island's proving grounds. Now all traces of the great iron target have disappeared, the only signs of activity being the seagulls which fly away at our approach.

For the past few years the caretaker of the island has been Edward McDevitt, with his wife and children. Ed enjoys the island named Peddock's.

The MDC now controls the island.

HINGHAM BAY

In 1637 the town of Weymouth was granted two islands in Hingham Bay: Grape Island, and what is now known as Bumpkin Island. The grant read as follows: "Round Iland & Grape Iland are graunted to the towne of Weymothe."

BUMPKIN ISLAND

Desiring to visit Round, or Bumpkin Island today, we pass through the swift waters of Hull Gut and continue in a southeasterly direction, soon approaching our goal. The island cannot be confused with any other in Hingham Bay, as its forty-eight acres of sloping terrain with the yellow hospital-building ruins at the summit give it a distinctive appearance.

Samuel Ward bought the island early in the seventeenth century, and his will, executed March 6, 1682, gave the "Island leying Betwixtt hingham and hull, called Bomkin Island unto the collidge; and my mind is that it be called By the name of wards Island." A year later he wrote that he wished it always to remain the property of Harvard College. The island was then appraised, and found to be worth eighty pounds.

It was valued in 1865 at $1200 and brought Harvard $50 a year, an amount which Shurtleff cleverly suggests "is fully equal to that yielded to Boston by the famous Franklin Medal Fund." Samuel Ward's daughter married a member of the Lobdell family of Hull; for many years the Lobdells lived on the island and paid rent to Harvard College.

The island passed from family to family, the acreage being used in the early part of the nineteenth century for drying fish, in addition to the usual farming. In 1879 the ruins of the old farmhouse could still be seen on the western side of the island, and an old wharf with rotten planks faced the channel. At this time, a well of excellent water was located near the wharf. Several stone walls that then crossed the property showed the extent to which the acreage had been farmed in olden times. Sweetser, in 1888, said Bumpkin Island was a "conspicuous, green dome, arabesqued with daisies and thistletops."

Perhaps it was this description which first influenced Clarence Burrage in his search for an ideal island for the children's hospital which he planned. He was so pleased with this island that he leased it for five hundred years and arranged title to erect a hospital building on the highest point of land. The first load of lumber for the structure was delivered in September 1901; working as a deck hand on the lumber barge was John A. Glawson. When the barge was unloaded, Arthur Bemis, Secretary of the Hospital Association, stepped up to Glawson and asked him if he would like to work on the island. Glawson accepted.

The hospital was ready for occupancy by July 1902, the first children then being admitted. Dr. Clarence Crane was the first physician in charge; the matron was Miss Bertha Carvell. Dr. Crane served for one year, after which he was succeeded by Dr. Thomas Strong. That year the hospital closed for the season in September, but Glawson stayed on with his wife during the long winter that followed. The wonderful work done by the Burrage organization will never be fully realized or appreciated; long summers on this delightful island did much to aid children in their battle to regain health. At one time as many as 145 children were registered and the hospital continued its work until the trumpets of war were heard.

In April 1917, Dr. Edgar, head physician at the Charlestown Navy Yard, visited Bumpkin Island and arranged that it should be used by the Navy for the duration of the war. Glawson was made watchman, sleeping on the sun porch with a shotgun for protection. The rumors concerning German spies did not make his sleep a peaceful one, but soon the sailors began to arrive and regular guards were installed. Glawson enlisted in June 1917 and remained at the island in a semi-official capacity.

At this time numerous sailors from Boston landed at Bumpkin Island, building after building being erected to house them. At the peak during the year 1918 there were over thirteen hundred sailors stationed here, quartered in fifty-eight buildings; Glawson could hardly believe it was the old familiar place. He was allowed to go ashore to his residence in Wayland every weekend, and it was after his arrival home on January 11, 1918, that he received word by telephone that water was freezing in the pipes at the hospital building. Since the Bay was frozen over at the time except for an occasional water hole, Glawson donned his heavy rubber boots and started out across the Harbor. Proceeding along the ice from Sunset Point, he thought he was far enough down the Harbor to avoid stepping into the open water just off Bumpkin Island, but the next thing he knew he was over his head in the Bay. Grasping at an ice cake, he managed to get his leg over its edge, and pulled himself up. This difficult feat saved his life, as no one could have reached him in time.

The first naval commander of Bumpkin Island was Captain James Porter, who was later sent to sea aboard the training ship *Nantucket*. John Cushing was the next captain in charge, staying at Samuel Ward's old home until January 1918. Commanding Officer B. H. Camden then assumed control until after the war was over.

A fine band of twenty-five pieces, led by Conductor Harris, did much to cheer the hundreds of sailors waiting for action at the island. Toward the end of the war they were given a bandstand located in front of the hospital building.

After the Armistice, the buildings were gradually torn down and either taken off the island and rebuilt, or the material was sold to the highest bidder. The commanding officer's house, built late in the war, was sold to John Duane of Quincy, who moved it to the mainland. The Knights of

Columbus building was given to Cardinal O'Connell, who moved it down to Nantasket Beach, where it still stands as an accommodation house for worthy people. The remains of the oil shed can be seen down near the dock, and the foundation of the cement mess hall still stands. Fifty-seven of the fifty-eight buildings were removed and the great hospital once more stood alone, silhouetted against the sky-line of Hingham Bay. After the war the island settled back to normal times, with Glawson once again becoming its head man.

Glawson made a splendid record in rescuing people from the sometimes turbulent waters of Boston Harbor. In this he had taken the place of the intrepid Captain Joshua James, whose record will probably never again be equaled. James died on March 19, 1902, and Captain Glawson made his first rescue shortly afterward. With twenty-eight rescues to his credit, Glawson can be said to have as fine a record as any inhabitant of the islands of Boston Harbor. There were three which he remembered most vividly. The first occurred in June 1907, when Arthur Lane chose to sail down the Harbor from the Quincy Yacht Club at Hough's Neck in spite of rough weather. Coming abeam of Bumpkin Island, his craft capsized and he was thrown into the water. Glawson rushed down to his boat, started the engine, and succeeded in reaching Lane before it was too late. The second rescue Glawson described occurred in 1921, after a sailboat from Lynn was struck by a vivid bolt of lightning. He reached the occupants before the boat sank beneath the waves.

In Glawson's opinion, his most unusual rescue took place in 1911. He and George James were towing a dead horse to Spectacle Island, where the rendering plant was located. Passing a small boat, Glawson noticed there were five boys on board, and a moment later over she went. Glawson now had what might be termed a busy half hour trying to rescue the frightened boys from the overturned sailboat, with the dead horse still towing behind. James gave valuable assistance, and soon all were safe aboard the Glawson boat.

A rather unusual addition to the captain's stories was enacted on the afternoon of Sunday, May 19, 1935, when the writer was visiting Glawson and interviewing him on his rescues. As the captain was relating some of his many experiences, he happened to look out over the water, just in time to see a small sailboat tip over with two boys. After a race to the dock, the writer, piloted by Charles De Gaust, was able to reach the boys and bring them ashore. They were Willis H. Bagley and John Pepi of Quincy.

Some odd items on the island may interest the reader. The only grave belongs to a horse. The island was formerly a smelting center, barrels of smelts having been caught right off the shore where there was still eel grass in the Harbor. Glawson remembers catching 720 in one day. The smelts disappeared when the eel grass vanished some years ago, and have only gradually returned. A bright red car of moderately old vintage purred contentedly about the island during the summer months, facetiously called by the mainland residents, the "Bumpkin Island Fire Department." It was brought across the ice during the severe winter of 1933–1934 and had an interesting identification sign painted on its side:

JOHN W. GLAWSON

CHIEF

OF THE

WHOLE WORKS

BUMPKIN ISLAND

MAGEE & KING   DEPUTIES

The yellow hospital building burned down many years ago.

GRAPE ISLAND

We now turn our attention to the other island mentioned in the ancient Weymouth grant, Grape Island. Thomas Jenner of Weymouth was one of the earliest men to own property on Grape Island, and he sold a small part of it in 1649 to Edward Bates. Joseph Green bought five acres of Grape Island in 1694. Samuel Thaxter, John Porter, and Jonathan Torry were part owners in 1722, and they all sold their shares to John Gould. The Ludden family were living at Grape Island between 1694 and 1725, James and Benjamin Ludden being property holders.

During the Revolution, the island was owned by a prominent Tory of Hingham, Elisha Leavitt. Realizing that the British officers needed hay for their horses quartered in Boston, he sent word for them to come down to Grape Island and gather the hay. When the British arrived, the alarm went around the mainland; soon the South Shore minute men were on the job, and the Red Coats were forced back to their boats. This glorified skirmish, which occurred on May 21, 1775, has gone down in history as the battle of Grape Island.

The notorious Captain Smith settled on Grape Island shortly after the close of the Civil War, and his life history is one of the fascinating subjects of Hingham Bay. Smith's real name was Amos Pendleton. He was one of the striking characters of the last century, ruling Grape Island in true piratical style. This old sailor of a forgotten day took many thrilling yarns to his grave when he passed on. At the age of nineteen he shipped aboard the *Golden Star*, a slaver bound for the West Indies, and was later promoted to first lieutenant. The ship was heavily armed, carrying sixty men and seven hundred slaves. One day the *Golden Star* encountered a British cruiser, the *Black Joke*, and after the flashing cutlasses were sheathed, the slaver had won a distinct victory. Over a hundred lives were lost in this encounter. When Captain Smith described the incident one could almost hear the cutlasses singing over his head. Smith later became a smuggler in the bayous near New Orleans. Finally, when the authorities made it uncomfortable for him, Smith fled to New England and settled on quiet little Grape Island. After such a life, it is no surprise to learn that he used to send bullets over the heads of any trespassers on the island. There is one account of a man who was wounded by a shot from his gun. Mr. Pierce Buckley of the Boston Public Library once heard the old man's voice a mile away, warning trespassers off the premises. But Amos Pendleton, alias Captain Smith, grew old and feeble, giving up his home on the isle in 1892. He died in the Hingham Poor House in 1897 at the age of ninety-two.

The care of the island until 1901 was in the hands of a mysterious gentleman whose name we must omit, as it is understood he had committed a serious crime in Boston. Because of certain complications with the city authorities, he retreated down the Harbor to avoid capture. When this gentleman moved to the mainland, Captain Billy McLeod and his wife became the caretakers of the island and lived there thirty-four years.

One day as Billy McLeod was strolling along the beach he found a tiny baby seal which he took into the house. The seal soon became attached to the family, and in a few weeks was performing feats of unusual agility. In the morning it flipped its way down to the shore, took a swim, and then returned to the house. It learned to knock three times with its flippers as a signal that it wished to enter the house. Once inside, it made a straight line for the stove, behind which a little box had been placed. Here the seal remained until suppertime. After supper Captain McLeod put a little rug in the box, whereupon the seal yawned in a knowing manner and curled up on the rug for the night. Whenever the captain returned from Boston, the seal swam out to meet him and climbed into the boat for the ride back. The little seal died from eating green paint, and many children who had visited the pet mourned its death. Captain Billy said that although he had owned many dogs since then, there never was an animal as affectionate as his little seal.

Living alone on the island, Captain McLeod and his wife had many adventures together. During the First World War two sailors knocked at the captain's door, asking permission to borrow his boat to reach the mainland. They had wrecked their skiff on the other side of the island and offered the captain a valuable watch as security for the boat. Billy McLeod decided they should spend the night at the house, so let them have shelter in the loft. Morning came and the sailors were gone—so was the boat. When Captain McLeod learned that they were deserters from Bumpkin Island, his only regret was that he hadn't taken the expensive watch for security.

One of the queer tales of the island is that of the gold mine. Over twenty years ago Billy McLeod discovered a woman and two men digging a deep pit on the other side of the island. When he ordered them to stop, they told him they were digging for gold. The woman professed to be a clairvoyant who had dreamed of gold buried on Grape Island. Whether or not they were the same people who dug for the treasure at Castle Island in 1911 is an interesting conjecture. When Captain Billy first told me the story, he said, with a twinkle in his eye, that the only gold found on the island was out on the flats where hundred and thousands of bushels of clams had been dug throughout the years. Even the Indians knew the secret of the real treasure of Grape Island, and countless tomahawks have been found in the piles of clamshells they left behind.

Billy McLeod was stone deaf due to an accident while sailing in the outer Harbor; the only manner in which we could convey our thoughts to him was by writing our message. Sometimes, especially if Mr. McLeod was not used to the handwriting, he misinterpreted the meaning, and this led to many amusing situations. In 1934 we visited him with a friend, Thomas Johnson of Winthrop. By various notes Johnson had found out that Billy McLeod was a former member of the South Boston Yacht Club, and he wrote out a question asking McLeod if he had ever met the great fighter, John L. Sullivan. "Never heard of him," was McLeod's astonishing rejoinder, whereupon I struck the well-known attitude the boxer usually assumed while posing for a picture. "Ah," cried McLeod, "you mean John L? I saw him many a time."

Another of Captain Billy's stories was about his wonderful Toulouse geese. These birds grew so smart that they would swim in and out around the smelt fishermen anchored in the Bay, asking for bait! McLeod did a wonderful business selling bait to the fishermen at the height of the smelting years. Around 1912 there were hundreds of fishing boats of all descriptions anchored all the way out past Boston Light. The days of good smelting seem gone forever.

Captain William McLeod passed away on February 28, 1935, shortly after a tragic accident that occurred while he and Mrs. McLeod were walking over the ice to the mainland. Hundreds of members of the Massachusetts Bay yacht clubs will remember this delightful old couple who were so hospitable during their thirty-four years at historic Grape Island. The ghost of Amos Pendleton must have been uneasy while watching the courteous reception the McLeods gave almost everyone who asked to visit the island.

SHEEP ISLAND

In Hingham Bay between Peddock's Island on the north and Grape Island on the south lies Sheep Island. It is occupied in summer and fall as a residence and hunting lodge. William Chamberlain was the earliest known owner of this island, having the property in his possession around 1650. His estate was divided in 1661, and Robert Coombs and his wife Sarah were granted Sheep Island sometime before 1686, for on March 8 of that year they sold the property to John Loring of Hull. He and Benjamin Loring, "yeoman," sold the island to the Chamberlain family. On July 22, 1735, it passed on to Ebenezer Chamberlain, at whose death John Henderson assumed control of its six acres. Henderson at once turned the property over to John Petel, Jr., who had married Eunice Chamberlain, the daughter of Ebenezer. A year later Eunice Petel transferred the title to John Doane. Elisha Leavitt purchased the island in 1765.

I am afraid the reader will not enjoy a further discussion of the different owners of Sheep Island, so we shall turn to the various titles it has been given. In the *Gentleman's Magazine* for 1775 it is called Sun Island. Another chart sixteen years before called it Shean Island, while Dearborn's Map of 1865 locates it with the title Sheaf Island. A very pretentious chart made about 1780 leaves out the property altogether, while including such comparatively insignificant ledges as Quarantine Rocks and Sunken Ledge. Still another name by which is was known was Ship Island.

We landed here in 1932, and perhaps the most striking feature we noticed were the giant decoys on the beach. Gunning on the island has of late been conspicuous by its absence. But in spite of the lack of birds we can say, along with the poet Thomas Dibden:

Oh, it's a snug little island!
A right little, tight little, island.

SLATE ISLAND

A mile to the southeast of Sheep Island, and just to the west of Grape Island, lies Slate Island, the quarry of the Puritan fathers. The Massachusetts Bay Records for October 16, 1650, mention the grant of this island to William Torrey, but the public was allowed to use the slate. Although twelve acres here have furnished hundreds of tons of slate, the quarry is seldom used at present. The property has been owned at various times by Joseph Andrews, Samuel Lovell, Thomas Jones, and Caleb Loring. It has been called Hat Island, State Island, and Slat Island. Around 1840 it was the home of a mysterious hermit who lived here for many years. Sweetser tells us that his lonely hut must have made Thoreau's hermitage at Walden look like Scollay Square after a theater performance. Very little is known of this recluse who chose the wilds of Slate Island in preference to life with his fellow men.

The island is owned by the Clapp Memorial Association. A generation ago the Boy and Girl Scouts were given permission to camp on the island in alternate months of the summer, and their white tents stood out against the dense foliage growing there. Mr. Clapp, the former owner, died in 1909.

RACCOON ISLAND

Three hundred yards off the eastern shore of Hough's Neck lies Raccoon Island. It was owned early in the eighteenth century by Edward Capin, but little of its history is known. In 1950 the Stigmatine Fathers, the former owners of the property, conducted their summer school on the island. The little chapel was very active from late June until early September. The 2600 feet of shore line were guarded by two giant dogs who were quite successful in keeping the island peaceful and quiet for the study of the Scriptures.

THE HINGHAM HARBOR ISLANDS

Sailing the route of the famous Hingham packets of years gone by, we pass down Hingham Bay, slip by Samuel Ward's old Bumpkin Island, then past Crow Point, and find ourselves in Hingham Harbor. Four pleasant islands dot this little bay, the first to be visited being Ragged Island. This isle, together with Sarah's and Langlee's, at one time belonged to the intrepid Captain Langlee. All three islands are delightful to visit. With its many coves and inlets Ragged Island is appropriately named. We quote a few lines from Bouvé's delightful description of 1893.

"This island . . . is a very picturesque mass of rock, and the scarlet and yellow of the sumacs and the other wild shrubs form a fiery contrast to the deep olive green of the savins here and there among the ledges. At half tide, the musty underwater coloring of the rocks of these islands supplemented by the dark, yellowish russet tints of the rockweed, which only grows submerged on the ledges, is very interesting in an artistic point of view."

Sweetser's artist drew a charming scene at Ragged Island with four mermaids sporting among the rocks. In 1880 there was a fine observation platform at one end of the property. The island is seldom used today except by the occasional yachtsman. A bridge once connected it with the mainland. Ragged Island is conglomerate puddingstone and slate, mixed with sedimentary and volcanic rock.

Passing across the narrow channel we reach the shore of Langlee's Island. The Langlees of Hingham are mentioned in the Massachusetts Bay Records for February 1685. This island contains the same geological formation as Ragged Island, and in very early times was known as Ibrook's Island. It is a beautiful spot, thanks to the excellent taste of the man who made extensive plantings here in the early nineties. Due south of Langlee's Island lies Sarah's Island.

There is an interesting legend concerning these three islands situated close together in Hingham Harbor. Mrs. Sarah Derby, according to the story, lived as a ragged young girl on the islands mentioned. When she grew older, they came to be called in her honor, Ragged Island, Sarah's Island, and Langlee's Island. It is a pretty story, but unfortunately a chart of the Harbor made in 1700 clearly shows that the islands went by those names at the turn of the century, while Sarah Derby was not born until 1714. However, a John Langlee of Hingham is mentioned in the Massachusetts Bay records of February 16, 1785, so possibly his daughter is the young lady in question.

About a third of a mile away lies Button Island, close to the site of the old pier where the Hingham packets used to tie up after their long trips from Boston. In spite of extensive research, the writer has been unable to find anything of importance concerning this small island. It has a few trees and shrubs but is so small that no one has considered it except for picnicking. Made of felsite diorite, it was brought to the surface due to faults in the earth's structure.

FORT DUVALL, LITTLE HOG ISLAND

Little Hog Island is the last to be discussed in this chapter. Although at the present time it is owned by the Federal Government, it was at one time the place where old ships, having outlived their usefulness, were broken up. Henry David Thoreau believed the whole island was "gently lapsing into futurity," and said that "this isle has got the very form of a ripple." When Sweetser visited the island in 1882 there were two wrecks on the beach where "myriads of spiders, large and small have carefully woven their silken webs across every corner." The names of the ships were the *Passport* and the *Virginia*.

Fort Duvall, a masterpiece of engineering, is on the island. Two sixteen-inch guns once stood at Duvall, but the isle is used for experimental purposes today.

11

DEER ISLAND AND
LONG ISLAND

'There are two islands in our Harbor which have become small towns in themselves. Deer Island and Long Island, with a combined area of four hundred acres, have a population of three thousand. This population is made up mostly of people under care of the city of Boston, the county prison being located on Deer Island and the almshouse and hospital on Long Island. Strictly speaking, Deer Island is no longer an island, for on the macadam road that connects it to the mainland, autoists may pass at any time of tide. Long Island, located across President Road from Deer Island, is more isolated, but is now reached by a bridge built in 1951.

DEER ISLAND

Thirty-five years ago we could visit Deer Island by boarding the *Michael J. Perkins* at Sargent's Wharf, Eastern Avenue, Boston. This dock, situated at the foot of Fleet Street, was known as Scarlett's Wharf when Captain Quelch and many other pirates were taken there on their way to be hanged. As we land at Deer Island, Deputy A. H. McCarthy greets us at the dock. Let us go up to the highest hill where formerly the signal flags relayed messages to Boston, and view the island which William Wood, in 1634, called "Deare Iland, which lies within a flight-shot of Pullinpoint."

Deer Island is over a mile in length and contains 183 acres. It is divided, as was Gaul, into three parts, the United States Government, the state of Massachusetts, and the city of Boston each owning a share. According to the latest survey, the national Government owns one hundred acres, while the city of Boston owns the larger part of the remainder. The United States Navy has a radio compass station at Deer Island, and the Government has other stations here. The House of Correction for Suffolk County is situated near Shirley Gut, and the Pumping Station for the Commonwealth of Massachusetts, North Metropolitan Sewerage District, is on the western side of the island.

Three hundred years ago Deer Island was overrun by the animals from which it gets its name. William Wood, writing in 1634, tells us that the "Iland is so called, because of the Deare which often swimme thither from the Maine, when they are chased by the Woolves: Some have killed sixteen Deare in a day upon this Iland." In April of the same year Deer Island, Hog Island, and Long Island were granted to Boston for two pounds rent, and the Province never set any further claim on the island. The rent was later reduced to the equivalent of twenty-five cents for each island.

The winter of 1634–35 must have been unusually severe,

for many men were marooned on the Harbor islands. Three wood choppers coming to Boston from Deer Island found the ice so thick that they had to stop at Bird Island for the night. The Harbor was frozen over several times in the year 1635.

The next year it was agreed "y^t ye Inhabitants who doe want wood, shall have liberty to gett for their vse, at Deare Island, so as y^t they psently take & carrye away what they doe gett, & whatsoeur they have felled there to be at liberty for others to take away." Five years later Deer Island was made the location of a pound for swine and goats found roaming around Boston. It was built by Edward Gibbons. In January 1642 it was ordered that Deer Island should be improved for the maintenance of a free school for Boston, and Daniel Maude, who succeeded Philemon Pormort as master of the Latin School, profited thereby.

The town of Boston leased Deer Island on December 30, 1644, to Elder James Penn and John Oliver for three years at seven pounds a year but allowed the inhabitants of Boston to cut wood at the island. Three years later Edward Bendell leased the island for seven years, paying double the small rent that his predecessors had been charged. He had some trouble in making his payment in 1655 but managed to extend the lease to twenty-one years.

In 1642 the *Mary Rose* had been blown to pieces "with her own powder" while coming up the Harbor, her hulk remaining in the channel, a menace to navigation. As much treasure had gone down with the ship, Edward Bendell worked out a device by which he could recover the wreck of the vessel. The Court made an agreement with him whereby if he could not move the ship he would receive half of any treasure he might find, and if he moved the hulk everything would be his. Bendell now constructed two huge water-tight tubs open at one end, turned them upside down, and weighted them with several hundred pounds of metal. He arranged a swing for himself inside the tubs, with two signal cords running up to the men who would lower him down into the sea. Bendell was able, by this arrangement, to stay under water for thirty minutes, a remarkable feat for colonial days. He salvaged the *Mary Rose*, brought her into shallow water, and received the treasure, but only after a struggle, as others had appropriated it for themselves.

In 1655 James Bill, a resident of Pullen Point, was barred from cutting wood at Deer Island since the authorities believed there was only enough to supply a farm. A little later John Shaw leased Deer Island, renting it in 1663 to Sir Thomas Temple who was reputed to be a direct descendant of Lady Godiva.

Temple leased the island to Samuel Shrimpton on December 4, 1668. When King Philip's War broke out in 1675, hundreds of friendly Indians were forced to move to Deer Island. A few months later, old Ahatton and other Indians petitioned for the right to visit other islands to get clams and fish, as the redskins were starving to death. Many did perish from hunger before a boat was provided for the unfortunate men. On the nineteenth of April, 1676, Jonathan Fairbanks asked possession of a certain little Indian girl who at that time was a member of a tribe on the island, but it is not known if his request was granted. Later in the war the colonists changed their attitude; Deer Island Indians were pressed into duty against the victorious tribes, and helped turn the tide for the Puritans.

After thus aiding the New Englanders, these Indians brought forward some of their old claims, and Charles Josias, alias Wampatuck, grandson of the great Chicatawbut, demanded the island. His claims were settled by compromise, and a group of prominent Bostonians including Shrimpton and Simon Lynde paid him nineteen pounds for his rights. Another Indian, David, son of Sagamore George, now told the Court he was the owner of Deer Island but gave up the claim after a few weeks of heated debate.

Deer Island was first suggested as a quarantine station on August 3, 1677, when the passengers of Captain Legg's ship were ordered confined "at an island such as Deare Island" because of smallpox on board ship. Forty years later it was again suggested that Deer Island be used for this purpose.

During 1688 Governor Sir Edmund Andros was trying to collect a tax from all landowners. When Shrimpton failed to pay him, Andros sent his High Sheriff, James Shurlock, down to Deer Island. Shurlock took John Pittom, the tenant, with his family, and turned them adrift in a small boat, leaving two men on the property to see that Pittom did not come back. This action was carried out even after the *supersedias*, similar to an injunction of today, had been served on him. If High Sheriff Shurlock had known of the flight of King James II from London during the preceding month, perhaps he would not have been so eager to follow the commands of Sir Edmund Andros.

Back in England, the Bloodless Revolution was on. William landed at Torbay on November 5, 1688, and William and Mary were proclaimed King and Queen of England on February 13, 1689. John Winslow brought news of these events to Boston on April 4, 1689. We know that Sir Edmund Andros had previous knowledge of the debacle, and this has perhaps influenced some of us to believe a legend about King James and Deer Island. The legend says that James asked Andros to pick out a likely place in Massachusetts Bay as a possible hideout for him until he could recoup his losses and that Andros chose Deer Island as suitable for the requirements of his ruler. Sir Edmund Andros did not count on the *coup d'etat* at Fort Hill under John Nelson which took place April 18, 1689; Andros was thrown into prison, and his plans, of course, were given up. The King of England at Deer Island!—such at any rate is the legend.

Colonel Samuel Shrimpton died on February 8, 1698, and his widow, Elizabeth, leased the property at Deer Island to Christopher Capron the next year. Very little is known of the island's history for the next eighteen years.

In 1717 the citizens of Boston voted to have the selectmen "Lease out a piece of Land on Dere Iland, not exceeding one acre, for a term not exceeding ninety-nine years, to be improved for the Erecting an Hospital or Pest House for the reception & entertainm^t of sick persons coming from beyond the Sea." Spectacle Island, however, was made the Quarantine Station of Boston Harbor in July 1717, and Deer Island had to wait over one hundred years before it was to receive the sick from incoming vessels.

During the Revolution Major Greaton of the Continental Army landed at Deer Island and removed several hundred sheep and a number of horses from under the eyes of the British fleet anchored less than a mile away. Another incident of more tragic import was the Battle of Shirley Gut on May 19, 1776. Although the British were finally forced to retreat, brave Captain James Mugford was killed. He had previously captured a much-needed British powdership for the Americans, bringing it to the American shore line. Waiting his chance to return to Marblehead, he sailed for Shirley Gut, but the British overtook and killed him in the battle which followed. The ship carrying his body safely reached Marblehead where Mugford was given a stately funeral.

The celebrated lifesaver, William Tewksbury, moved to Deer Island shortly after the Revolution, making his first rescue in 1799. In December of that year he saved an English sailor who had fallen from a vessel anchored in the Harbor. The following year Tewksbury rescued a sailor from the masthead of a schooner which had crashed off Fawn Bar. At this time he was assisted by his colored servant, Black Sam, who later drowned in Shirley Gut. In March 1809 this Deer Island hero earned another medal by taking Thomas Gould from the masthead of his pickey boat, wrecked on Winthrop Bar. The Tewksburys ran an entertainment and picnic resort here for many years.

On May 26, 1817, Tewksbury made his most outstanding rescue, one which made him known from Boston to Baltimore. At four o'clock the afternoon of that day, he and his son Abijah were collecting ballast near the present site of the Winthrop water tower when a boy from Point Shirley came running up the beach to tell them that a pleasure boat had upset somewhere between Deer and Long Islands. Tewksbury and his son rushed to their canoe, hoisted sail, and soon reached Shirley Gut. As Tewksbury could not see the wrecked boat, he stood for Long Island until he saw his wife and children running along the beach in the direction of Money Bluff. He then changed his course to run parallel to theirs. As the wind was blowing strong and he had already shipped a barrel of water, Tewksbury was greatly discouraged to see what appeared to be twenty or thirty heads bobbing up and down in the water about a half mile off the shore from the Bluff.

The canoe was a small lap-streak model, a heavy sea was running, and Tewksbury's wife and children were watching him from the shore. He realized that his own chances of reaching safety were small, but he took in his sail and managed to get seven of the eight survivors into the frail canoe. The eighth man was anxiously awaiting his turn when Abijah called to him, "Father, the canoe is sinking, we shall all perish." Tewksbury had been so interested in the rescue that he had not noticed the water steadily creeping up the sides of the boat; by the time the seventh man was aboard the water was within three inches of the gunwales. Therefore he had to start for Deer Island without the last man, who was holding onto the jolly boat tied to the sunken pleasure craft. The canoe with its nine occupants safely made shore, but when Tewksbury returned for the lone mariner, the man had vanished. Evidently the tide had risen just enough to submerge the jolly boat so that it was of no use to the unfortunate sailor. Three others had perished before Tewksbury arrived. Those saved had been in the water not quite an hour. The Reverend Mr. Brown describes the final scene in this unusual rescue:

> *The suff'rers they at length receiv'd,*
> *Then hasten'd to the shore;*
> *In hopes that those might be reliev'd,*
> *Who seem'd to breathe no more.*

> *And ere the sun had sunk below*
> *The surface of the main,*
> *They felt their grateful bosoms glow*
> *With life and health again.*

For his heroism Tewksbury was rewarded with a gold medal from the Massachusetts Humane Society.

Again in August 1820 Tewksbury made a difficult rescue. While he was at breakfast, he received word from Mr. Wyman at Point Shirley that a boat had sunk on Fawn Bar. John W. Tewksbury, William's cousin, helped launch the frail canoe in the heavy northerly sea, and they were soon sailing in the direction of the wreck. They found the lone sailor, William Morrison, straddling a part of the gunwale of the boat which had gone to pieces in the surf. Morrison said that after his boat had crashed onto the bar it had broken up and drifted into deep water. After three weeks on the island, he recovered sufficiently to return home. Five other people were rescued by Tewksbury's son the same year. Up to 1825 the Tewksbury family had saved thirty-one lives, and had received numerous medals.

In the 1830s there was a peculiar tragedy at old Pullen Point when a baker, apparently in the last stages of alcoholic insanity, drove down to the Point in his buggy and shouted that he was going to cross the Gut at high tide. Whipping up his horse, he drove into the swirling current where horse and man quickly drowned. It was remarked at the time that the loss of the man was not serious, but it was to be regretted that he had taken along a dumb animal in his folly.

The signal station at Deer Island was attended in the year 1819 by the Rev. Frederick William Augustus Steuben Brown, wandering poet of Boston Harbor. His summer there must indeed have been a fascinating one, and his visits doubtless occupied most of his spare time, for his poetry has the factual background which could have been acquired only after careful research. He is reputed to have been one of the founders of the Methodist Church in Winthrop, and was often seen in the company of Sturgis the salt manufacturer.

Six verses of his poem on Deer Island follow:

> *Here superstition often tells,*
> *Of ghost, that's heard to screech,*
> *And utter dismal piercing yells,*
> *At midnight on the beach.*

For oft I've heard the story told,
  How a ghost without a head;
Here guards some thousand pounds in gold,
  By some strange fancy led.

          • • •

Ye sons of festive mirth and dance,
  To Tewksberry's hall repair;
His kind attentions will enhance,
  Your pleasures while you're there.

There shaded by some willow trees,
  The bowling alleys lay,
With seats, where you may sit at ease,
  When not inclin'd to play.

When not inclin'd to dance or sing,
  Upon a lofty tree,
There hangs a strong, well guarded swing,
  From ev'ry danger free.

Which, swiftly through the yielding air,
  In steady, lofty flight,
Will gentleman or lady fair,
  Convey, with pure delight.

The Shade of Alden, James Lloyd Homer, visited Deer Island in 1845, spending many happy hours bowling on the green and swinging young ladies in the picturesque swing by the trees. He tells of a curious treasure hunt that turned out to be unsuccessful. In 1824 a group of men, including Captain Tewksbury, Rev. Mr. Brown, and Captain Crooker, went down to Money Bluff where they dug silently for several hours, but did not find even one coin. Captain Crooker blamed the failure of the expedition on some of the party who talked after promising to keep silent. It had broken the spell!

When the terrible ship fever raged among the Irish immigrants in 1847, Dr. Moriarty was placed in charge of the temporary quarantine established at Deer Island. Hundreds of immigrants stricken with the fever died there and were buried in nameless graves. The Quarantine Station at Deer Island was made permanent in 1849. In the same year plans for a new almshouse were drawn, and this building, completed in 1852, is in use even at the present time as part of the prison.

Paupers of the city and commonwealth were soon removed to the new building at Deer Island, and on January 25, 1854, it became the House of Industry. Before the year elapsed, the Massachusetts poor were sent to Rainsford's Island, and on July 1, 1858, the inmates of the House of Reformation together with those of the almshouse school connected with it were sent to Deer Island. In 1869 a farmhouse was built and a house for pauper girls was also constructed.

The bar which runs out from Deer Island was the scene of a shipwreck in the winter of 1886. At daybreak on January 9 the schooner *Juliet* crashed against Fawn Bar. The ship had sailed safely from the Mosquito Mountain Quarry in Frankfort, Maine, into the outer Harbor, but the snow was so thick that Captain Leach misjudged the channel, and the ship ripped up on Fawn Bar Ledge. Heavily coated with ice, she rolled over on her beam ends, with the men trying desperately to hang on. Three of the crew, Hollis Munson, Philip Truesworthy, and Winnie Milliken, having lashed themselves to the mast, were forced to watch the other three gradually lose their holds and be swept off the ship. The breakers, twenty and thirty feet high, rushed over the vessel, engulfing everything for four or five seconds at a time. The first to be lost was Charles Truesworthy, the mate; the next to die was one of the crew, James Dunn; and the last to lose his life was Captain Leach. At 9 A.M. the sea had gone down enough to permit the tug *Samuel Little* to come to the aid of the survivors. Four inmates of the prison assisted in the rescue of these men. The granite from the cargo of the *Juliet* still lies near Fawn Bar.

The Suffolk County House of Correction was moved to Deer Island in 1896, while Master James R. Gerrish was in charge. The previous year the reformation department had been transferred to Rainsford's Island. The Hill Prison and the power plant were built while Gerrish was master at the island. Gerrish is said to have advised against the location, believing it too near the water. When Gerrish resigned in 1907, James H. Cronin became master. In 1910 a new seawall was built near the Hill Prison, but three years later it was badly in need of repairs. In November 1920, a storm destroyed 450 feet of the wall, and Commissioner Johnson secured an old barge which he floated up on the beach for protection. Emergency repairs were made in 1925, and a permanent wall was later constructed.

Major George F. A. Mulcahy, a Dartmouth graduate and First World War veteran, was appointed master of Deer Island House of Correction on September 16, 1926.

A prison break was attempted on August 14, 1933, when four prisoners drove across the Gut at low tide, using one of the island trucks. Making the wrong turn at Point Shirley, they abandoned the car and hid. The writer happened to be at the Point, and his car and services were commandeered by four guards, two of whom rode on each running board with riot guns in their hands. All the prisoners were finally captured and returned to prison.

William C. Ham of Winthrop, who as a boy lived on

Deer Island, enjoyed many interesting experiences in connection with the island. In 1895 he was the first to travel through the new pipe laid under the Gut, and in 1932 was in the first automobile to drive across the Gut at low tide. He also had a thrilling experience during the great storm of 1898, when the frame of the house which he had just left floated off and out into the ocean after a great wave swept around it.

Shirley Gut started filling up years ago. It has been claimed that the *Constitution* sailed through this narrow passageway in 1812, but none of the books about this famous American ship mentions the fact. As late as 1895 the Gut was navigable by the Nahant boats, but around 1920 the depth at high tide was only six feet. Ten years later it was only half that depth, and by the summer of 1935 only a few inches of water were to be seen except at the highest tides. For the first time in history Deer Island is connected with the mainland, with a macadam road now connecting Point Shirley and Deer Island.

Receiving Officer Kenny once wrote the first chapters of the history of Deer Island, but abandoned the idea and tore up the manuscript because of the great amount of work involved.

Resthaven Cemetery at Deer Island, established in 1908, stands for much that is romantic and tragic in the history of our islands. Although many of the inscriptions have disappeared because of the admitted activities of certain South Boston young men in 1892, I have been able to trace many of the people whose remains were there until 1939.

The body of John, who while at Castle Island was a "desperate good Gardener," is still buried at Deer Island. The quotation is from his gravestone, now lying at the bottom of Pleasure Bay. Edward Pursley, who died at Castle Island in 1768, was interred here. Shute Bernard, the son of Sir Francis Bernard, and Sir Thomas Adams were at Resthaven, where their remains were moved from Castle and Governor's Islands. Lieutenant Robert F. Massie's gravestone was here, beside that of Edward Johnston, the Confederate sailor who died while at Fort Warren. The body of Johnston was also at Governor's before being taken to Deer Island. The remains of those who perished in the Castle Island mine explosion of 1898 were here, as were recently found Confederate graves. All are now at Fort Devens in Ayer.

DEER ISLAND LIGHT

We shall now visit Deer Island Light, located five hundred yards from Deer Island, and a thousand yards from Long Island. This lighthouse has had its share of romance and tragedy. Keeper Wesley Pingree spent his honeymoon here with his bride, the former Josephine Horte, in 1896. Frank P. Sibley, First World War correspondent of the *Boston Globe*, lived at the Light several summers in the 1890s, and his acquaintance with Miss Florence Lyndon, daughter of Keeper Lyndon of Long Island Light, resulted in their marriage in 1893.

Wesley Pingree's worst experience while at Deer Island Light was during the *Portland* storm of 1898. Former Keeper Pingree's account of that terrible November night follows:

"At two o'clock in the afternoon the ocean was as smooth as glass. At 5 P.M. it had started snowing hard, and the wind was coming up. A little later the Bangor boat went by but returned to the harbor, as the sea was rapidly getting worse, at 7 P.M. the *Portland* came down the channel, and the other boat, anchored in President Road, whistled a warning to her. At this time the waves were hitting so high I was up lashing my dory fast to the Light. The *Portland* continued right out to sea, and as she was lost with all hands, I do not think she was ever seen again."

Another tragic story is more intimately connected with the Light. Keeper Joseph McCabe had left the Light one winter Sunday in 1916 to help his fiancee at Deer Island address their wedding invitations. In the afternoon the temperature dropped, and a howling northwester sprang up; when McCabe reached the shore at the Island he found his boat frozen to the beach. As it was low tide, he borrowed rubber boots and started to walk along the bar to the Light. Jumping to a large rock while approaching his goal, he slipped and fell into the ocean. Watchers on the shore quickly launched a dory, but they reached the spot too late.

Judson B. Small became the assistant-keeper of Deer Island Light in 1923. Merrill B. King was keeper when Small started his service, and during the gale of December 27, 1930, was at the Light alone. At 4 P.M. that day breakers forty feet high were sweeping right across the mile-wide area between Deer and Long Islands; every time a sea hit the lighthouse the whole structure would shake. Keeper King had previously calked cotton in all the cracks through which water might seep. Being alone at the Light in such a storm was a fearful experience, but when morning came the worst of the blow was over and the sea subsided by noon of the next day.

Judson Small's brother Tom had been keeper at Bug Light until the fire of 1929, when he was transferred to Duxbury Pier in Plymouth Harbor. Merrill King left Deer

Island Light in June 1931, being succeeded by Tom Small. Riprap put to the eastward of the Light somewhat breaks the force of the sea during a gale, but there have been rumors to the effect that the foundation of the lighthouse is weakening. A telephone connection with Boston enables the men at the Light to notify the Chamber of Commerce when ships are sighted down the Harbor.

The present keeper at the Light is Tedro Marticio.

LONG ISLAND

Leaving Deer Island Light, we cross over to Long Island, the longest of all the islands in Boston Harbor, although it does not have as much shore line as Peddock's.

In the early part of its history, Long Island was closely allied with Deer and Hog Islands, being granted on April 1, 1634, along with the other two for three pounds to the town of Boston. The rent was changed on March 4, 1635, to four shillings, with Spectacle Island added. On February 24, 1640, the one and thirteen-sixteenths miles of Long Island were laid out in lots for planters. This was done at a Boston town meeting at which "Edward Randsford & Will-yam Hudson are appointed to accompany ye surveyor to laye out the planting ground at Long Iland, & they are to beginne at the East end." A pleasant philosophy is expressed in the following rule laid down at this meeting of 331 years ago, to the effect that "if any have bestowed any labor vpon y^t wch shall fall to another man, he whoe shall enjoy ye benefitt thereof shall eyther allow for ye charge, or cleare soe much for ye other."

We have seen various instances where islands have been claimed by Indians, but few controversies between white

men are recorded. One of them is in Liber I of the Suffolk
Deeds where we find the record of "a protest against intruders Edward Tomlins and Timothy Tomlins with
Hansard Knowles Clarke and others by James fforrett gentl
and signed by John Winthrop." The island had been
granted, according to the protest, "bu the letters Patents of
o^r Sovereine Lord Kinge Charles to the Right Honora Will
Earle of Sterling," and the intruders had settled there in
spite of the grant. Regardless of this claim, which was filed
on September 28, 1641, the Right Honorable William, Earl
of Stirling, was never recognized as the lawful owner of
this island.

The planters of Long Island remained there almost eight
years after Earl William tried to evict them, but on April
19, 1649, they were notified that a yearly rent would be
charged for the benefit of the free school at Boston. Thirty-
seven people now bound themselves to pay sixpence an acre
every year, and as there were some two hundred acres that
could be cultivated, a sum of about five pounds was annually
realized in this manner. In 1655 the farmers at the Island
fell behind in their payments, and the constable was ordered
to collect the overdue rent. Affairs went from bad to worse,
until on March 11, 1667, the town of Boston told the tenants at Long Island that if they paid up their back rent they
could have their lots without further payment.

Let us delve a little into the Suffolk Deeds of this period.
Joseph and Elizabeth Rock owned at least forty acres of
Long Island in 1669 and mortgaged this land in 1671 for two
hundred pounds. The mortgage was paid off on August 9,
1672, the same day that the Rock family sold eight acres of
property to James Brading. These eight acres were in two
different sections of the island, bounded on the west by
property owned jointly by Edward Cowell and Jonathan

Balstone while the Bastond family owned the section due east, the Harbor being the north and south boundary. Nathaniel Reinolds and Gamaliel Waite also were tenants at the same time, owning property respectively due west and east of the second section. The above-mentioned names would seem to include a majority of the landholders of Long Island in the year 1682. The language of the deed which conveyed the property to James Brading should be of interest: "2 parcels of land with houses, outhouses, Barnes, Stables, wharfes, yard's, Orchard's, garden's, Meadowes, Marshes, Pastures, feeding's Wood's, Vnderwood's water's, fishings, profits etc." Just what was left for the "etc." to include is a question.

Property owners at Long Island at this period were James Woodward, Susanne Compton, Edmund Brown, Richard Tailor, and Thomas Stansbury. Stansbury, a shopkeeper of Boston, held onto his property longer than any of the other tenants, whose land was gradually bought up by John Nelson, relative of Sir Thomas Temple. Nelson's daughter married Robert Temple of Noddle's Island, and their granddaughter was the mother of Robert C. Winthrop.

On April 18, 1689, Nelson headed a band of colonists at Fort Hill and ordered Sir Edmund Andros to surrender himself and the fort. This revolution led to the imprisonment of Andros at Castle Island. When William was firmly established on the English throne, the colonists who had participated in this first outburst against authority probably breathed more easily. What would have happened to them had James II returned to power is another story.

John Nelson became so prominent an owner that by 1720, thirty-one years after the storming of Fort Hill, Long Island was still known as Nelson's Island. In the meantime much had happened to Nelson. He had started on a voyage in 1692, was captured at sea by the French, and imprisoned at Quebec. While in prison in this northern settlement, he discovered that the French were plotting against the New England people, so he secretly dispatched a messenger to Boston to warn the colonists. When the French learned of Nelson's trick they sent him to France, where he was locked up in the Bastille. Only after years of effort by Sir Purbeck Temple was he released. When he finally returned to Long Island, he was given a wonderful home-coming banquet to celebrate his arrival. He had been away ten years, and the celebration was so important that, according to Sweetser, fragments of the table cloth used at the feast were still preserved in 1880!

When John Nelson died on December 5, 1721, at his island kingdom, his estate was divided into seven parts. Robert Temple bought up four of these shares, and then he and the other owners conveyed the whole island to Charles Apthorp. Apthorp died in 1758, and his heirs sold the entire island of 216 acres to Barlow Trecothick, the lord mayor of London. Trecothick had married Grizzell Apthorp, the eldest daughter of Charles W. Apthorp.

When Lord Mayor Trecothick died in June 1790, Charles Apthorp became the owner of the island. He kept it barely a year, selling out to James Ivers of Boston, who died in 1815. Ivers left two daughters, Hannah and Jane. The first mentioned had married Jonathan Loring Austin, while Jane had become the wife of Benjamin Austin. Four years later the Long Island lighthouse was built. The tower, erected on the highest part of Long Island Head, was twenty-two feet high and could be seen for fifteen miles. It has been moved twice since its erection in 1819.

Thomas Smith of Cohasset bought the entire island in 1847, and when the Portuguese fisherman started to build shacks there, he sold it to the Long Island Company, which was incorporated in 1849.

When James Lloyd Homer visited Long Island Light in 1845, he found Captain Charles Beck, already with many years of service, in charge of the lighthouse there. Beck explained to him that when a pilot boat in the Harbor had run out of pilots, the captain hoisted a blue and white ball as a signal, whereupon Captain Beck raised a black ball from his mast to let the officials in Boston know of the situation in the outer Harbor.

Ballou's Pictorial for December 27, 1856, carries a picture of the Eutaw House at Long Island. It was a "commodious building and pleasant resort," according to the legend accompanying the picture. I have been trying to find out whether the Eutaw House became the Long Island House, but have not as yet had any success. We do know that during the Civil War the Long Island House was used by the soldiers quartered on the island.

The first regiment to be quartered at Long Island was the famous "Fighting Ninth." This regiment was recruited by Thomas Cass, formerly commander of a Massachusetts Militia organization known as the Columbian Artillery. Composed almost wholly of men of Irish birth, six of the companies were from Boston, and one each from Salem, Marlboro, Milford, and Stoughton. After a long tedious stay at Faneuil Hall in Boston, the soldiers were taken aboard the *Nellie Baker* on May 12, 1861, and soon arrived at Camp Wightman, Long Island. The camp was named in honor of Mayor Wightman of Boston. Pickets were set up along the shore to prevent desertion and interference from sailing craft, and the soldiers soon began to feel they were actually in the army.

Drilling became the event of the day, and as all were

anxious to master the manual of arms, this led to a pleasant duel of ability between Sergeant-Major Teague and Lieutenant McCafferty. Teague announced one day that he was McCafferty's equal, so a contest was arranged to see which was the better. Although Teague gave an expert exhibition, Lieutenant McCafferty's wonderful work with the musket soon showed he was the master, and Teague was the first to congratulate him. Lieutenant James E. McCafferty was later killed in action at the battle of Gaines' Mill, Virginia.

A few weeks after the Ninth arrived at Camp Wightman, another regiment was quartered on the western side of the island, about a half-mile away. Many of the officers started the custom of visiting this new regiment at night against orders. When Colonel Cass learned one evening that some of his line officers were missing from camp, he had the countersign changed while the officers were still out. The colonel heard the officers returning and walked down to the sentinel they would have to pass, keeping in the background. The guard, knowing the colonel was close at hand, changed to "charge bayonets" and loudly called "Halt! Who goes there?" This so astonished the returning officers that they halted and ceased talking. One of them called out that they were friends with the countersign, and tried to give the word. He failed, of course, and when Colonel Cass stepped forward, the officers knew the game was up. They were each inspected by the colonel, and after a severe scolding, were dismissed.

On June 11, 1861, the 13th Regiment, M.V.M., became the Ninth Massachusetts Regiment, U.S.V. Company A came to be known as the Columbian Guards, as there were many who had belonged to the old Columbian Artillery, established in 1798. Company B, or the Otis Guards, was named in honor of Mrs. Harrison Gray Otis. The Douglas

Guards, Company C, was named for Stephen A. Douglas of Illinois. Company C quickly became known as the Meagher Guards, thus honoring the Irish orator and exile who later became the great General Thomas Francis Meagher of the Army of the Potomac. Company E was named the Cass Light Guards, in honor of Colonel Thomas Cass. Company F was known as the Fitzgerald Guards, for Lord Edward Fitzgerald, the Irish patriot. It had been recruited in Salem. Company G, from Marlboro, or the Wolf Tone Guards, was named for Theobald Wolf Tone, one of the founders of "United Irishmen." Company H, the Davis Guards from Milford, was named for Thomas Osborne Davis, Irish poet. General McClellan was honored by Company I, from Boston, which was called the McClellan Rifles. K Company from Stoughton became known as the Stoughton Guards. Thus we can understand the character of the ten companies assembled at Long Island on June 11, 1861. On Monday, June 24, 1861, friends of the Ninth Regiment presented the organization with an American flag and an Irish flag, both made of silk. On one side of the green Irish flag, under the American coat of arms, a scroll bore the following inscription: *Thy sons by adoption; thy firm supporters and defenders from duty, affection and choice.*

The reverse side contained the Irish harp; below the harp were two wolf dogs and the motto: *Gentle when stroked, fierce when provoked.*

At 2 P.M. on June 26, 1761, the Ninth Regiment sailed from Long Island. Friends and relatives had come down to make their final farewells, and as the boys marched up the gangplanks and on the three steamers there was no cheering; the occasion was too serious. The *Ben de Ford*, the *Cambridge*, and the *Pembroke* were the three ships selected to carry the 1022 men to Washington, and as the transports sailed into the channel and passed Long Island Light, a last view of the deserted tent city was presented. For many of the men it was the last view of Boston Harbor. Thus we leave the Ninth Regiment on its way to the front.

With the year 1863 it was seen that there would have to be conscriptions for the army. After several other sites had been abandoned, a great conscript camp was finally established at Long Island, because of the difficulty of escape from this refuge. General Charles Devens, the commanding officer there, certainly had his hands full trying to keep the conscripts in order. His headquarters were at the Long Island Hotel, which was opened especially for the occasion, with the officers under him quartered in the spacious building. Other officers included Captains Goodhue, Leach, Clark, Goodwin, and Hughes, and the surgeon was Dr. N. M. Hayward.

Some of the adventuresome conscripts believed that they could escape to the mainland, one such attempt taking place on the night of Sunday, September 13, 1863. Four conscripts deserted in a small boat and, by skillful navigation, managed to go part of the way to another island before their makeshift craft sank in the channel. Two were drowned, but the other two men were successful in reaching Jeffries Point, East Boston. They were soon captured and brought into court, where nearly $1000 in money was found on them. When the bodies of their companions were picked up, $408 was taken from their pockets. The names of these deserters had best go unmentioned.

The steamer *Bellingham*, the official conscript boat in charge of Captain Lovell, made one especially pleasant trip to Long Island during the time it was in service. On October

9, 1863, there was a great picnic for non-commissioned officers and privates of old regiments who were guarding the conscripts at Long Island. The wives and sweethearts of the men were included and enjoyed the dress-parade and clambake which followed. One unhappy incident occurred in the evening when a deserter was removed from the *Bellingham*. He had been placed in the guard house, and in some unexplained manner escaped and secreted himself on board the boat.

At the end of the war Long Island returned to the peaceful pursuits of former years. In 1867, however, an important change was effected when Fort Strong, Noddle's Island, was moved down the Harbor to Long Island Head. This was permitted by an act of Congress approved on March 28, 1867. As the various owners of the land on the island would not come to terms with the Government, two decrees of condemnation were necessary. The first was for 35.39 acres against J. T. Austin and Loring H. Austin, and the other for 14.29 acres against Peter Dunbar and Thomas Dunbar. These men were the survivors of the Long Island Land Company crash.

The island gradually became the place for Sunday prize fights, and many fistic encounters were witnessed at old Camp Wightman. The police finally had to stop the pugilistic activities of Sunday visitors, and on June 29, 1873, when a riot squad of forty husky policemen landed on the shore, there was a great run for the boats. Some escaped and some were captured; at any rate this put an end to the Sunday prize fights for many years.

The Portuguese families had been quietly living at Long Island since 1850, but the city of Boston decided to take over the island, except for the fifty acres owned by the Federal Government, and made the purchase in 1882. In

1887 the city of Boston was forced to evict the thirty Portuguese families then living at the island; they took up new abodes around the Harbor. The male paupers from Rainsford's Island were moved to Long Island in 1895, and the female inmates of the almshouse at Rainsford's Island were also moved there.

The late Pierce Buckley of the Boston Public Library had an experience involving Long Island of the 1890s which almost caused his death. He had obtained an old sailing canoe and had left South Boston with another youth named Lyons. They sailed joyfully out into the Harbor, across the channel between Spectacle and Thompson's Islands, and coasted off Long Island until they were almost abeam of the lighthouse. Suddenly, over they went. Both clung desperately to the canoe, kicking their way toward shore. Reaching the island, they climbed up the hill leading to the lighthouse, but the keeper of Long Island Light told them in no uncertain terms to get off the island. The boys, shivering and wet, furled their sails, climbed back into their canoe, and paddled off toward South Boston where they finally arrived more dead than alive.

In the year 1899 extensive plans were made by the Government, and 15.24 acres were purchased from the city. These plans necessitated moving Long Island Light, and the work was begun on September 13, 1900.

For many years around 1900 the Randage Fund Excursion had picnics at West Bluff, Long Island. Rainsford's Island was also the site for many of these gatherings enjoyed by unfortunate children of Boston.

With the advent of the First World War about fifteen hundred men were quartered at Fort Strong, mostly those from the 55th Artillery. Captain Augustus L. Hodgkins had many a trying experience running the *Batchelder* around to the forts during the terrible winter of 1917–18. Perhaps his worst trip was during the night that Private Pratt lost his life. A bad northwest blow was on and it was bitter cold. Eight or ten men at Fort Andrews had to reach Fort Strong that night. It was so rough that a stop at one of the other islands had been abandoned. As the boat neared the dock at Long Island the deckhand, Private Pratt, came out on the windward side of the boat and walked over to the lee side. Heavily dressed in boots and mackinaw, he was lifted right up into the air by the force of the wind and dropped into the water. Life preservers were thrown after him, but he was not seen again. A year later his body came to the surface within two hundred yards of the place where he was lost!

On January 8, 1918, Edwin Tarr, keeper of Long Island Light since 1909, died while sitting in his chair looking out over the water. A soldier who was stationed at Fort Strong on Long Island during the First World War was one of the pallbearers at his funeral. The funeral was held in the old building then attached to the lighthouse. Before the funeral ended a terrific sleet storm began and transformed the hill where the lighthouse is into a gigantic ice-coated drumlin. The four unsuspecting pallbearers, with military precision, carried the coffin out the door and toward the path that led down the hill.

Suddenly one of the soldiers skidded, the coffin went down onto the ice, and the four men were forced to grasp the handles of the coffin and get aboard as the casket began traveling down the hill over the ice. Thirty seconds later the casket—which had become a toboggan—ended its weird trip down the hill at a point just near the head of the wharf. This former member of the 241st Regiment told me he would never forget his unusual experience.

Edwin Tarr was the Light's last keeper. The beacon was lighted by custodians until 1929, at which time it was made automatic.

Going ashore at Long Island in the year 1934, one could visit efficient Dr. Clay, who was in charge of the Long Island hospital and almshouse. Charles Lancaster Clay, Dartmouth '19, lived with his wife and four children in a residence to the left of the pier, with the various buildings of the institution situated south of his home.

The institution building, the men's dormitories, the women's dormitories, the men's hospital building, the women's hospital building, the chapel, the powerhouse, and the recreation center which came to be known as the Curley building were among the edifices on the island. The almshouse division and the hospital division are under the same general management, only minor differences being made between them. The Long Island Hospital is used for chronic diseases only. The hospital has about 490 patients, while the almshouse has over 890 inmates. There are so many people in the almshouse department that one of the Fort Strong buildings belonging to the Government has been leased by the city. Inmates of the institution are there voluntarily and may leave whenever they wish.

Meals at the island are important. Although John Moriarty, superintendent of the House of Industry in 1859, reported that he believed the diet list could not be improved, if the authorities were to sanction such food today it would cause a Congressional investigation. Breakfast then consisted of bread and chocolate, the dinner usually soup, and the supper merely bread and tea! In 1862 the report said that food furnished was "good and wholesome," but it implied there should be a change. A suggestion was made "to give milk to eat at times," and the question was asked if "the allowance of butter at least once a day, with an occasional biscuit would not do much to soften the inmates' dispositions and subdue their natures." The directors, however, did not believe the suggestion a wise one.

Until a number of years ago one could see along the shore quite a few small huts and camps made from driftwood washed in from the ocean. Many of the inmates of the almshouse occupied their leisure moments building and taking care of these huts, which seemed to take them away from the realities of life. We often paddled close along the shore to observe the fine gardens some of the men made, and noticed the fishing lines waiting for stray flounders or mackerel. Over thirty-five of these little cottages could be counted on the north and south shores of the island.

Dr. Fredcrick A. Washburn, later city of Boston Commissioner of Institutions, was commanding officer at Fort Strong, Long Island, during the First World War. While there, a communistic individual was made to kiss the flag publicly. The incident was so distorted that by the time the story reached Boston it was claimed the man had been courtmartialed and shot. It is a curious turn of fate that placed Commissioner Washburn in charge of the Government end of the island at one time, and later on made him head of the department controlling the city end of this same island.

When I returned from North Africa during the Second World War, it was my pleasure to lecture at Long Island, where I met genial Doctor James V. Sachetti, Superintendent of the hospital.

The bridge to Long Island was dedicated by Secretary of Labor Maurice J. Tobin on August 4, 1951, making it much easier to reach the island, especially in winter.

The Long Island Chronic Disease Hospital was established in 1969. It is a combination of Boston City Hospital, Long Island Hospital, and Mattapan Chronic Disease Hospital along with Boston's Department of Public Health. Thus the actual name Long Island Chronic Disease Hospital came into being.

The Trustees of Health and Hospitals have made a definite commitment of $2,000,000 to renovate patient facilities consisting of 220 beds and are planning additional patient care renovation of 120 patient private and semi-private rooms. A new building for a kitchen and dining facility is planned at a cost of $1,500,000, with construction to begin in 1971.

Originally Long Island was serviced by boats coming from the North End of Boston. With the opening of the bridge from Moon Island to Long Island and with the commitment of these improvement funds by the city of Boston, the future of the hospital is assured.

As Assistant Director Edward L. Tyler, Jr., told me on February 5, 1971, the important people at Long Island Hospital are the patients. Patient care of the highest caliber has been a tradition of the staff of the Long Island Hospital, and, of course, only dedicated persons can carry out this important work.

Commissioner Andrew P. Sackett, M.D., has on his staff Dr. David S. Sherman, the Director of the hospital, who is also Assistant Deputy Commissioner. Assistant Director Edward L. Tyler, Jr., is among the most active executives at Long Island today.

Although I do not believe in ghosts, I enjoy hearing stories about them, and so it was that I invited Bill Liddell, a former soldier at Fort Strong, to go down the harbor with me in 1950. We landed at old Fort Strong just before dusk.

As we sat down on the cement apron at the top of Fort Strong I was fascinated by William Liddell's account.

Bill explained that during the British occupation of Boston in the Revolution, many Tories were confronted with the necessity of leaving Boston should the British forces move away. Then, in early March 1776, General Washington occupied Dorchester Heights and the British made plans to evacuate Boston by sea at once.

By Sunday, March 17, the "largest fleet ever seen in America" was in Boston Harbor, loading troops and refugees, according to Abigail Adams' diary. "Upwards of one hundred and seventy sail" were counted from her vantage point at Penn's Hill, Braintree. The ships had aboard 8,906 officers and men and 3,124 refugees. But only seventy-eight vessels sailed away on March 17, the others anchoring a short distance out to sea from Long Island.

There were soon only thirteen British craft left in the harbor. On June 13, 1776, American soldiers landed on Long Island and Nantasket Hill to begin a bombardment of the British warships still in the bay.

Aboard one of the British craft were Mr. William Burton and his wife Mary. Mary had become friendly with three other women, and on the day the bombardment started was visiting their quarters. The first cannon ball that hit the ship passed through the open port and mortally wounded Mrs. Burton. Still conscious, Mary pleaded with her husband.

"I know I'm to die, William, but please don't let them bury me in the sea. Please, William, bury me ashore. Promise me, William!"

William promised her that he'd take her ashore at nearby Long Island and there dig her grave. Burton obtained permission to go ashore a short time afterward under a flag of truce.

Soon the longboat was ready for the trip. Sewn into a red blanket, Mary's body was placed in the boat and William landed with her remains at Long Island Head. At the top of the hill William met the American gunners and explained his mission.

A brief service was held, after which Mary Burton was buried. One of the soldiers agreed to put her name on a gravestone. William and the crew soon launched the longboat and reached the warship, where the captain had been anxiously awaiting their arrival. An hour later they sailed, and landed at Halifax the following week.

Of course, Burton planned to return to Boston as soon as the rebels were overcome, but years went by and then came the surrender at Yorktown. By this time Burton knew that he would never return, and he died at the turn of the century without visiting the grave.

Back at Long Island, however, the soldiers had placed the wooden headstone over Mary's remains, but by the time of the surrender the headstone had rotted away, and those who knew the story erected a cairn at the location.

In 1804 a group of fishermen were wrecked at Long Island in a storm, but managed to reach shore safely. Climbing the cliff, they found shelter in the old powder storage magazine at the fort, where they attempted to build a fire to keep warm. As they knelt down over the fire, they heard a strange moan or wail coming from over the brow of the hill, near the cairn.

The sailors went to the entrance of the casemate, where they again heard the moan. Then they saw the form of a woman wearing a scarlet cloak coming over the hill. It appeared as though blood was streaming down her cloak from a terrible wound in her head, but she kept on walking, soon disappearing over the hill.

Again during the War of 1812 the Woman in Scarlet appeared at Fort Strong on Long Island, but the Civil War passed without her appearing even once. She appeared in 1891 before Private William Liddell. She came toward him from an easterly direction, and her moaning was quite distinct. When I took William Liddell down to Fort Strong in 1951, he pointed out the exact spot where he had stood when the ghost came over the hill, moaning and wailing.

12

ISLANDS OF THE OUTER HARBOR

Although Little Brewster, the smallest of the Outer Islands, has more written history than the others of the Outer Bay, we find that all the islands and ledges scattered around near Boston Light have considerable romance and charm of their own. There is much to attract the traveler to Green Island, Calf Island, Great and Middle Brewster, and last of all, Outer Brewster. Off by itself, a mile and a half to the northeast from Green Island and slightly farther to the north of Outer Brewster, lies Graves Ledge, which we shall first discuss.

GRAVES LEDGE AND LIGHT

This ledge was named for Thomas Graves, an early Puritan who was captain of one of Winthrop's ships. Shurtleff insists that the rocks were called Graves to honor Captain Graves of Revolutionary War fame, but the chart of

Thomas Pound, drawn well before 1700, clearly shows that Shurtleff's assertion is impossible, for even then the ledge was known as the Graves. Some have claimed that the ledge was named because of the many sailors who were supposed to have drowned near by, but they are mistaken. There is no record of a shipwreck here until long after the ledge was named. While a few wrecks have occurred on these lonely rocks, in no case does the loss of life approach that sustained in the vicinity of Boston Light. The only large ship that ever crashed here was the *Ewan Crerar*, which hit the Graves on March 9, 1860.

The ledge in the outer Harbor came into prominence soon after the start of the twentieth century, when it was chosen as the site for the lighthouse that was to be built to facilitate entering the newly-opened Broad Sound Channel. After the 776 granite blocks had been safely put in place and the huge frame of the light itself had been sent out on a barge and installed, the beacon was lighted for the first time on September 1, 1905. It was a first order Light, the only one of its class in Boston Harbor.

The first keeper, Elliot C. Hadley, who had been transferred from Plum Island, found it a lonely station, as there was no telephone, radio, or TV at that time to help pass the evening hours. The telephone cable was brought out to the Graves during the First World War, and a radio and TV were installed some years ago.

Hundreds of people have visited Graves Light, but the first time the trip from Winthrop to the lighthouse was completed in a canoe was in 1906. This journey almost ended in death, not from the ocean, but from the piercing rays of the sun. Three men were the pioneers in the Winthrop-Graves Light trip: Howard Gould of the *Boston Traveler*, Walter Kezar, and Albert Morris. It was on a

Sunday morning that they left Winthrop Beach for the ledge, a day that turned out to be one of the hottest of the summer. Before they reached the Light, Kezar was badly burned. On their arrival at the ledge, Captain Hadley noticed Kezar's inflamed skin and gave him a thin sweater to wear on the way back to Winthrop. By the time they neared Winthrop, Kezar was in agony and when they landed on the beach he was rushed to a hospital, where he was found to be suffering from third-degree burns. His life was in danger for some time, but he finally recovered.

In the six years that Elliot Hadley spent at Graves Light there was one major disaster. On November 21, 1908, a small fishing schooner, the *Hugh G*, sank in a collision near the ledge and all six of the crew were drowned. At another time a scow in tow went down, but the tugboat saved the crew. One day in the fall of 1910 Hadley was surprised to see two men floating by the ledge on an overturned canoe. He launched his boat into the northwestern gale that was blowing, finally reached the unfortunates, and pulled them into the dory. Clad in bathing suits, the two men presented a dismal appearance when they were taken from the water. They had left Salem that morning and were on the way to Cohasset when the gale struck them. Hadley brought the men back to the Light, outfitted them with some spare clothing, and sent them ashore the next day. He later found that the men had been contemptible enough to give him false names, so that he never recovered his clothing.

Another rescue Hadley made is well remembered. The keeper was looking out to sea from the deck of the Light one day when he spied a swamped sailing boat drifting out to sea. Hastily launching his dory, he rowed out to the boat and succeeded in rescuing the occupants. Back on shore the relatives of those who had been saved had given up hope, and since there was no telephone at the Light, Hadley could not inform the mainland of the rescue. Great was the rejoicing the next day when the rescued party was safely brought back to the city.

In the days when Hadley was keeper, he and his son spent half of every month ashore while the assistant keepers took care of the Light.

Keeper Hadley was interviewed at the Light in 1910, and discussed the various directions from which the storms approach the ledge.

"The Graves doesn't get pounded so hard in a Northeast as an Easterly, and Southeast is the worst. . . . I've stood on the bridge and looked up at solid water rushing in toward the ledges. I don't know how far up the solid water comes. I've been knocked down by it on the stone wharf beside the Light, and opening a window to look out eastward more than halfway up the tower, I've had as much as three buckets-full dashed in my face. The seas never shake the tower."

Hadley resigned as keeper of Graves Light on September 22, 1911. Up to that time he had received many awards from the various humane societies of New England and was the proud owner of a gold watch given him for saving a grateful resident of Nahant. Elliot Hadley died a generation ago but will always be remembered for his fine work at Plum Island and Graves Light.

George Lyons, who had twenty-one years of experience on Egg Rock, Nahant, became the next keeper. After two years of service, he was succeeded by Captain Towle, who stayed at the Light until America entered the First World War. Keeper Carter took over Graves Light on July 31, 1917, and observed Armistice Day while still in charge. Seven years later he resigned in favor of Captain P. S. King, who was at the Light less than a year. Octavius Reamy, well-known South Shore photographer, took charge on May 11, 1924. He and his two helpers, First Assistant Fitzpatrick and Second Assistant Rogers, kept the interior of Graves Light as neat as the most meticulous housewife could desire. I visited Graves Light many times and always found everything in perfect order.

In one of the heaviest fogs of 1936 the steamer *New York* crashed into the *Romance*, off Graves Light, and although no lives were lost the *Romance* went down in twenty minutes not far from Graves Light. In the spring of 1938 the *City of Salisbury*, a 419-foot freighter, its decks crowded with wild beasts, struck a sunken reef near Graves Light. The crew and most of the animals were taken off safely, but considerable cargo was lost. All that summer hundreds of sightseers made the journey out to what they called the "Zoo Ship," but when the turbulent winds of an October gale swept up the coast the great ship rolled over and disappeared beneath the waves. It had been the most spectacular shipwreck in Boston Harbor history.

The fishing schooner *Mary E. O'Hara*, early on January 21, 1941, passed Graves Light inward bound, and headed for Deer Island Light, a beacon she was destined never to reach. It was bitterly cold. Suddenly there was a terrific crash, and the *O'Hara* sheered off, settled, and went down in forty feet of water. The fishing schooner had struck a barge anchored near Finn's Ledge. The frightened men scrambled up the rigging into the crosstrees, which were still above the surface of the sea. The surf froze on the shivering sailors as they clung there, hoping for rescue, but help failed to come in the blackness of that January night. One by one the discouraged men abandoned all hope, slipping off the mast into the icy water, until only five of the crew of twenty-three remained alive. With the coming of dawn the trawler *North Star* sighted them and picked up the survivors. This tragedy was the third worst shipwreck in Boston Harbor history.

A little more than ten years went by. Then, at twenty minutes after five on the night of Wednesday, November 29, 1951, the 10,000-ton tanker *Ventura* was sailing out of Boston Harbor. Suddenly, without warning, she crashed into the stern of the tiny 170-ton *Lynn* a relatively short distance from the location where eighteen fishermen drowned from the *Mary E. O'Hara* in 1941.

The man at the wheel of the *Lynn*, John J. King, was in the pilot house with Mate Jim Hayes and Captain Carl McNamara. John Rogers had just entered the wheel house to suggest that the captain join the others at supper when they heard the bell of another ship. Captain McNamara signaled for slow speed ahead, and all present peered out into the darkness, but they could see nothing.

As Captain McNamara turned to tell King to alter his course, he saw to his horror the forward lights of a ship looming up dead astern. Grabbing the signal, he pushed it to full speed ahead. Just then there was a slight bump, not too pronounced, and the *Lynn* was heeled over and engulfed under the hull of the great towering *Ventura*. The trawler, with thirteen men below at supper, was pushed over on her side and down under the *Ventura*'s keel.

The men at supper didn't have a chance. Not one of them was ever seen alive again, but the four men in the wheel house were thrown clear as the larger ship simply rolled the trawler under.

The four men in the water were eventually rescued, but two of them, Hayes and Rogers, died after being taken from the sea. Captain McNamara and King were the only ones

who survived. King explained later the *Lynn* had flipped
over like an eel. The force of the water had thrown him
back and jammed him against the door of the pilot house.
King managed to get through one of the open windows in
the pilot house. Just then the *Lynn* went down and King
went with her, drawn by the suction. Coming up to the
surface, he could hear the shouts of others, but they seemed
far off and then died away. After floating for some time
King was rescued and taken back to Boston.

The *Lynn* was located under water and the following
year was brought to the surface under dramatic conditions.
While not one of the worst disasters in Boston Bay, the loss
of the *Lynn* was one of the most heartrending and needless,
for although the night was dark the visibility had been
good. Fifteen men lost their lives in the collision off the
shores of Winthrop, Massachusetts.

In the winter time the rock plovers call at Graves Light
and feed on barnacles attached to the rocks. Hundreds of
them settle on the ledges which at low tide stretch out for
a quarter mile, and the keepers find the birds an enjoyable
diversion. The plovers feed by driving their long, sharp
beaks into the barnacle shells and seem to keep quite happy
on this menu. The men have taken some very interesting
photographs of these birds and of winter life in general at
the Graves.

We shall now sail out to the ledge, hailing the officer in
charge from our boat. If he is not too busy, he will invite
us "aboard." There is a wharf built in back of the riprap,
placed here when the Light was erected, with a long runway going from the storage magazine to the lighthouse
proper. We anchor on the lee side of the ledge and row
ashore.

The keepers help us up onto the wharf. We now get a

close view of the lighthouse itself. The date, 1903, which is cut in the granite, stands out in sharp contrast about fifty feet up on the stone edifice. Climbing a heavy copper ladder on the western side of the lighthouse, we reach the first stage, forty feet above the wharf. On this level we see the cover to the cistern, which is thirty-five feet deep and holds hundreds of gallons of water. The tank is filled twice yearly with water brought out to the Light by steamboat. The second stage is the engine room, where two semi-Diesel engines are ready for an emergency. The third level is the kitchen, neat and clean at all times. The fourth staging is the bunk room, with two double bunks. The fifth floor, containing the library, is also the watch room where the men spend their leisure time before retiring. The quarters are very cosy, the telephone and radio serving as connecting links with the mainland. The sixth stage, or lantern floor, holds the mechanism of the Light, while the Light itself occupies the two floors above. We may go outside on the highest deck, and view the wonderful picture which unfolds itself. I shall not attempt to give you a description of the scene from the top of the Light but hope that some day you may journey to this far-flung ledge and see the splendid view for yourself.

BUG LIGHT

Bug Light, formerly a lighthouse but now only an automatic beacon, stands at the entrance to the Narrows, guarding the Spit, a bar that runs from Greater Brewster Island. It is less than a third of a mile across Black Rock Channel from Lovell's Island and almost a half-mile from Fort Warren. Built back in 1856, the original Bug Light stood until 1929 to warn the mariner of the dreaded Harding's Ledge, four miles to the southeast. The lantern was about thirty-five feet above sea level, and when a sea captain brought Bug Light in range with Long Island Light, he knew he was clear of Harding's Ledge and could safely enter the Harbor.

Although the romance of this lighthouse is now a thing of the past, we can recall a small group that once occupied Bug Light, so named "because of its many legs." In the year 1893 Gershom C. Freeman was given the position of keeper at Bug Light, succeeding the bearded Captain Turner. Three years later Mrs. Frank Tenney became his house-keeper, moving to the lighthouse with her six-year-old son Francis. In 1908 her son attended English High School, each day making the long row around to the lee side of George's Island from which he took a boat to the city. If a bad storm came up, he would stay on George's Island till the weather abated; otherwise he returned in the dory.

Mrs. Tenney well remembered the *Portland* storm. She had been digging clams on the bar that afternoon, and there was no sign of the blizzard then on the way. The Light successfully withstood the terrible gale that came up that evening. The stones striking against the iron legs of Bug Light played weird tunes for the occupants above in the light-house, as every upright was keyed to a slightly different pitch.

Tom Small was the last keeper of Bug Light. On June 7, 1929, he was painting the woodwork of the house when his blowtorch tipped over; the blaze that followed destroyed the Light. The lighthouse board voted against rebuilding the structure, erecting an automatic bell and light in its place.

In the summer of 1934, Ralph Keller of Point Shirley was cruising by Bug Light and noticed that the automatic machinery of the station was ringing the bell as usual every twenty seconds, but in a tone pitched two or three degrees higher than usual. He went ashore, where he found to his surprise that a seagull had built its home inside the bell, and that the nest had actually changed the tone of the bell. The mother seagull chose a rather startling place to bring up her young, with the monotonous tolling of the bell sounding more than four thousand times every day.

The future of Bug Light seems entrusted to the gulls. When we visited there in the summer of 1935 to walk the bar from Bug Light to Boston Light, I disturbed hundreds of gulls comfortably resting on the end of the Spit. Except for the casual trips of island sightseers, these birds will find undisturbed rest as the new keepers of Bug Light beacon.

One can no longer walk the bar, as dredgers cut away a large section of it.

MINOT'S LIGHT

Although Minot's Light is not officially in Boston Harbor, it has been an integral factor in the city's development, and so, perhaps, a few paragraphs on the Minot's Ledge Lighthouse would not be out of place here.

In 1847 the first lighthouse on the ledge was built to a height of seventy-five feet, at a cost of $30,000. It was an octagonal tower, resting on eight wrought-iron piles sixty feet high and eight inches in diameter. The piling, secured in many ways, was considered perfectly safe. The beacon was lighted on January 1, 1850. The welcome Light flashed for over fifteen months.

But a storm that began on April 15, 1851, turned into a hurricane by the next day. Keeper Joshua Bennet had gone to Boston a few days previously, and returned to the shore to find the gale increasing so quickly that he could not start for the lighthouse. His two assistants, Joseph Wilson and Joseph Antoine, had seen part of the wooden framework wash away on the morning of April 16, and were anxiously awaiting what the darkness would bring. That night, which was to be their last on earth, they lighted the Light as usual. The residents along the shore remember seeing the flashing beam as late as one o'clock the following morning, but when dawn came the structure had disappeared. At low tide the jagged edges of the piling, bent and broken, were visible a few feet above the ledge. The two keepers had been lost.

The Government soon made plans for a more substantial edifice at the ledge. After several years of preparation, the lowest stone of the new lighthouse was put in place on July 11, 1858. This stone and six others were actually laid under water at low tide. During the first year of work only 130 hours could be spent at the ledge. The work was under the direction of Lieutenant-Colonel Barton S. Alexander of the United States Engineers. The new Minot's Ledge Lighthouse was lighted for the first time at sunset, November 15, 1860, and was visible for sixteen miles. The flash, one-four-three, has led to the name, Lover's light, with the I-love-you balancing the count. The flash is now automatic.

THE BREWSTERS

The Brewsters were named for the children of Elder William Brewster of Plymouth. Let us discuss a little of the topography of this group of islands.

Greater Brewster is the highest island in the outer Harbor, its northern bluff rising 104 feet above high water. The southern bluff has been almost washed away and is not quite 50 feet high. Some 585 yards to the north lies Calf Island, its seventeen acres rocky and fairly low in the water. Away to the eastward in a straight line stretch Middle Brewster and Outer Brewster, both very rocky and surrounded by stony ledges. Outer Brewster is perhaps a few feet higher than Middle Brewster, and is a larger island, containing seventeen acres as compared with twelve for Middle Brewster. Green Island's single acre, with its rocky slopes, has a fairly steep cliff on the northern side and is separated from Little Calf Island by Hypocrite Channel. It is almost due north of Calf Island.

These islands of the outer Harbor were given to John Leverett in appreciation of the work his father had done for the struggling colony. On October 19, 1652, all the islands from Nahant to Allerton were given to the son of Governor Leverett who died on April 3, 1650. This grant did not last long, for Hull objected so strenuously that the Court finally passed the islands back to Hull, giving young Leverett five hundred acres elsewhere to compensate him for the loss of his Boston Harbor property. Captain Coomes of Hull now became the owner of the Brewster Islands, keeping them until the year 1686.

The pirates were very active in this period. One incident of 1665 makes us realize just how strong and bold they had become by that time. Captain John Prentice of Boston reported on July 8, 1665, that two days earlier he had been chased all the way across the Bay and right up to the Brewster Islands by these seventeenth-century buccaneers. The pirates gave up the chase as soon as Captain Prentice's ship passed Outer Brewster Island, and the captain duly reported the incident when his ship's cargo was discharged.

In 1686 Coomes sold the islands to John Loring of Hull for the equivalent of twenty dollars. The islands were gradually subdivided, and in 1700 all the property owners met and agreed that Great Island (Greater Brewster) should be

Bounded to the Steep Bank and the Wood should be Reserved for the Security of the Bank, and it is agreed upon that
if any of the outside lots did Wast By Reason of the Sea yet
as to feed for Cattle theay should have as good Rights as any
other Lots. That the other three Islands should be in a Second
Division and Bounded from Sea to Sea and that it Should be
Cleared in a General way a man for a lot to Cut down the
Brewsters and if any man did neglect or refuse so to do he
should Pay to the rest of the Proprietors 2 Shillings a day for
every days neglect.

Evidently Green Island was too small and rocky to come
in for consideration. It was also agreed that if any wood
remained standing on any of the islands in question by
March 31, 1708, it would become common property. With
such agreements in force is it any wonder that our islands
lost their forests so soon?

GREATER BREWSTER ISLAND

In 1681, on the highest part of Greater Brewster Island, the
town of Hull placed a beacon and received eight pounds
from the Council for the land so used. In 1726 a well was
dug two hundreds yards away, by Captain Hayes, the
keeper of Boston Light. Although the well gave fine water
for over two hundred years, it has now been abandoned.

The Lorings, the Goulds, and the Bosworths were prominent owners of land on the Greater Brewster in the early
and middle 1700s. John Jenkins bought a large part of the
property on April 26, 1774, and the following October
made the unusual gift of his share of the island to the
Second Baptist Church of Boston. The Reverend Isaac
Skillman, who was the preacher at the time, valued the
property at eighteen pounds. In 1792 the church, owning

twenty-nine thirty-seconds of the island, voted to lease it for any term of time. When James Brackett of Quincy desired to buy the island, he was informed an outright purchase was not to be considered, but he could lease it indefinitely. He chose to take full advantage of this offer, and leased it from February 8, 1817 until February 8, 2816, or for a period of 999 years, paying one hundred and fifty pounds. His son Lemuel, sold the island to the city of Boston for $4,000 on November 23, 1848, but we cannot tell if the sale took into consideration the fact that it was still owned by the Second Baptist Church. Possibly in 2816 the church will again own one of Boston's Harbor islands.

Honorable Benjamin Dean rented Greater Brewster from the city for many years and around 1875 moved a large house there from Long Island.

Ambitious plans were made by the Federal Government in 1898 for a torpedo chute to be installed at Greater Brewster Island. Since the Spanish War ended before any definite steps had been taken, nothing was ever done about it.

Very few ships have been wrecked on the shores of Greater Brewster Island. The *Clara Jane* piled up on the shore on February 1, 1898. In command of Captain Robert Maloney, the *Clara Jane* pounded on the beach for two days but did not go to pieces and was finally pulled off and repaired. There was no loss of life.

George H. Hatchard of Hull was interested in the purchase of Greater Brewster in 1911, and was willing to pay the city of Boston $6,000. Since the arrangement Mr. Hatchard suggested was not found acceptable by the city authorities, Boston kept the island until the First World War, when the national Government took it over.

John Nuskey became keeper in 1925, and before he was in charge, John Sandstrom reigned over the summer inhabitants for thirty years. Russell Lowry of Lynnfield now owns Greater Brewster Island.

MIDDLE BREWSTER ISLAND

Around 1840, fishermen moved to Middle Brewster. Augustus Russ, visiting here shortly afterward, became interested in the island, which he finally bought in 1871. Russ was known all over New England as the principal founder of the Boston Yacht Club. A few years later his friends called him the King of Middle Brewster Island.

In 1890 Benjamin P. Cheney and his wife, the former Julia Arthur, moved to a little house on Middle Brewster Island. In the summer of 1891 Cheney desired an ice-house, but, as he had only bought a house lot on the island, Russ did not wish him to put up an additional building. Cheney therefore moved off the island and purchased Calf Island outright.

When Russ died in 1892, the island was sold to Charles Adams, who soon sold it to his brother Melvin. Melvin O. Adams thought so much of Augustus Russ that he had a tablet sunk into the rock on the side of the residence on the property. I copied the legend on one of my trips there:

IN LOVING MEMORY OF

AUGUSTUS RUSS

Born February 6, 1827   Died June 7, 1892

Lord of this isle for twenty years

Generous, brave, and true in the hearts

Of his friends he reigns still supreme.

MELVIN O. ADAMS   POSUIT 1905

An interesting log book, begun by Augustus Russ and containing names of many notables who visited the island, is now in the possession of the Adams family. Incidentally, one of the Narrow Gauge ferryboats was named *Brewster* in honor of the island.

The flag staff at the Calf Island end of Middle Brewster once bore an inscription which told us Richard S. Whitney erected it here in 1902.

CALF ISLANDS

Calf Island is probably named for Robert Calef, who was prominent in early Boston and in Lynn history. The property was also called Apthorp's Island, and a sentence in the files at the Suffolk Court House, dated January 16, 1713, is of interest in this connection. Mention is made of Robert Calef having a "mortgage by me made of the premises to Mrs. Suzan Apthorp for 150 pounds."

It was some years after this time that a ship, driven far off her course, crashed on the rocks near here, the crew of seven losing their lives. The men were buried on the island, but nothing can be found as to who they were, or what ship it was that foundered there. There is one explanation possible—that the bodies were from the *Maritana*, which crashed on Shag Rocks in the year 1861.

Twenty-five years after the wreck of the *Maritana* another ship met a tragic end on Calf Island when the *Mollie Trim* ripped over on the ledges on January 9, 1886. This vessel, under Captain Christian Olsen, was heavily loaded with coal and bound for Rockland, Maine. When the gale blew up, he tried to make Boston Harbor and slid in between Outer Brewster and Green Island, finally going ashore at Calf Island. Olsen, when the ship hit, ordered the crew into the rigging, and climbed to the masthead himself. When the masts fell he was thrown clear onto the beach, and, after a few moments of unconsciousness, was able to get up and survey the position of the ship. To his horror the bodies of the four men of his crew came floating in to shore. After pulling them above the raging sea, he walked up to the home of a fisherman living on the island. When the waves finally went down the fisherman rowed him over to Boston Light, where a signal was set for aid. The tug *Emily* soon came to his rescue and took him up the Harbor, where he was transferred to the police boat *Protector*. The four members of the crew were Lennan H. Murphy and three men whose first names were Charles, Jacob, and Frederick. Their last names and their addresses were never known, so somewhere perhaps, even today, there are three families who do not know what happened to their boys.

Julia Arthur moved here in 1891, living in a handsome residence which her husband built for her at great expense.

Wanting Calf Island and Little Calf Island during the First World War, the Government paid Julia Arthur's husband, Benjamin P. Cheney, $46,500 and took possession. Augustus Reekast, known as Gus Johnson, was caretaker for years.

We called at Calf Island many times in the summer and fall of 1934. Mrs. Grace Reekast entertained us while we were ashore. We visited the lonely graveyard at the top of the island where the sailors were buried so many years ago in unmarked graves. The driftwood on the shore was piled up ten feet high. A Belgian police dog, Gyp, chased the many rabbits over the island and announced the arrival of visitors. Mrs. Reekast was quite busy with a new little baby, whom Gus called his "Little Periwinkle."

Walking about Julia Arthur's former mansion, we saw the large stage which she had in the great hall. One little tragedy we noticed was that of two little swallows which had evidently flown into the house through the chimney and had not been able to find their way out again. They were lying on the floor of the hall with their beaks just touching each other—dead.

Little Calf Island, barely an acre in area, is a rough, rocky ledge, and as far as can be ascertained, never had any history worthy of mention. Hundreds of seagulls have their nests here, unmolested except for the casual visit of some adventuresome soul from the mainland.

The island is now privately owned.

GREEN ISLAND

We know very little about Green Island. On the older maps it is called North Brewster Island. The fact that it is referred to in 1788 as Greene's Island makes me believe that Joseph Green, a well-known merchant of this period, either lived here or owned the property. There is not much to the island, however, as its single acre of rocks and soil does not permit development of the site.

Nathaniel Shurtleff tells us of Samuel Choate, who was rescued from this ledge in the Minot's Light storm of 1851. This lonely old man had been living here as a hermit, existing on lobsters, fish, and clams. He returned to the property after the storm, and it was not until 1862 that he was in trouble again. At this time his boat went to pieces, and he was taken up to Boston. Returning with a new boat, he was able to remain there three years more, but on February 8, 1865, he was removed for the last time as he was practically starving to death. Since he had no relatives, he was taken to the Bridgewater Almshouse, where he died a few weeks later.

About the year 1905 two fishermen named McFee and Johnson moved to Green Island. Every four or five days they would go to Boston with a great load of lobsters. After these fishermen left, a Mr. Young lived there for many years. The last and only house on the island was destroyed in 1932 when the crew of a boat wrecked on the shore built a fire to keep warm. The wind shifted and the house burned down. Andrew and Freeman DeGaust leased Green Island for three years at fifty dollars a year. They were the last fishermen to have the island.

The only dwellers on the island are casual fishermen who go ashore to sleep while their shipmates continue to Boston to sell their catch. The wreckage of many craft is still to be seen around the island.

OUTER BREWSTER ISLAND

Outer Brewster Island is, perhaps, the prettiest of all the islands of Boston Harbor. A day spent at this site of chasms and caves will never be forgotten by the visitor. It belonged with the other Brewster Islands in the early days and was not considered as a separate entity until after 1750. At that time it was known as the Outward Island. Some charts call it the Little Brewster.

Samuel Wait of Charlestown was one of its owners toward the end of the eighteenth century. When Mr. Wait died in 1790, his son-in-law, David Wood, inherited the property, estimated to be about ten acres at that time. The island was worth $400 on August 21, 1799, when Nathaniel Austin bought the property. After Austin's death in 1817 his son Nathaniel eventually acquired the whole island. In 1843 his brother Arthur W. Austin purchased the property and began his plans for macadamizing roads in Boston from material cut at Outer Brewster. At the same time he was cutting a canal through the outer part of the island as a possible anchorage for ships in rough weather. The demand for the stone material dwindled and the work stopped. Some say the decrease in demand was due to the progress of the railroads. It is believed that Elliot Street in Boston is still surfaced with material from this island, and a building near City Square, Charlestown, is known to have been partly built with material from Outer Brewster.

During the Civil War a fisherman by the name of Jeffers moved to the island with his wife and children. He built a shack on the shore near what was known as Rocky Beach and began his practice of trapping lobsters. All went well until one stormy November night when Jeffers and two companions were trying to land on the rocky shore after rowing from Middle Brewster. As anyone knows who has landed at Outer Brewster, there is no real beach, and the sailor who must reach the shore on a stormy night is in a serious plight.

The dory went down; two of the three men, including Jeffers, were drowned. When the survivor reached the rocky shore and told Jeffers' wife what had happened, she made the best of the situation, continuing to live at the island with her children. Finally she was forced to give up the unequal struggle and moved to the mainland. Hoodlums from the city soon destroyed their home on Rocky Beach.

The Honorable Benjamin Franklin Dean purchased Outer Brewster in 1871 for $1,000, and twenty years later Augustus Reekast, Sr., moved there. Mr. Reekast brought up eight children on this lonely place.

With the turn of the century Josiah Stevens Dean took charge of the property, and Mr. Reekast moved to Middle Brewster Island. The island was leased in 1909 by Mr. Freeman DeGaust, a lobster fisherman, who paid a yearly rent of eighty dollars. He had come to the United States from Canada at the age of sixteen.

One of the first steps Mr. DeGaust took was to erect on the island a sign reading: *This is private property; 10 cents a head for landing.* When engineers were measuring the channel, they had occasion to land at Outer Brewster to take their bearings, so one of them went ashore to negotiate with Mr. DeGaust. The outcome was that the latter agreed, for seventeen dollars, to let the engineers land whenever they wished; and he soon received his check from the Government.

Leading down to the water, Mr. DeGaust had a wharf three feet wide and sixty feet long, with a ladder at the end of the pier. A mooring about two hundred yards from the wharf accommodated his ship except in the worst blows from the west, when Mr. DeGaust would have to use another mooring on the other side of the island. During the years spent at Outer Brewster Island, Freeman DeGaust lost five boats from various causes.

One morning about six o'clock Mr. DeGaust was putting up his flag when he heard a shout; looking down from the cliff, he saw two men swimming in the water near a capsized dory. He rushed to the edge of the bluff and was amazed to see a third man swimming under water, approaching the cliff. He hurried to his boat and rowed to the spot, but the man had disappeared. The first two men successfully reached the shore. The body of the drowned man was found one month later, six hundred yards from the place where he had last been seen. Mr. DeGaust told me that the weird effect of the drowning man swimming toward him under water gave him perhaps the worst sensation he has ever experienced.

When the Government desired to purchase the island in 1913 the sole objection which the army representatives raised was the insufficiency of fresh water to supply the number of men needed to man the proposed armament properly. Mr. DeGaust always had plenty of water for the use of his family from his sixteen-foot well, but whether the supply would suffice for a larger group was a matter for conjecture. Arrangements were completed on June 4, 1913, when Outer Brewster Island became the property of the Government, which paid Benjamin Franklin Dean, 2nd, $2500 for the property. The construction of fortifications was carried out during the Second World War.

This island is crowded with enchantment and beauty, and down through the years, various writers have extolled its virtues. Shurtleff tells us that its cliffs far surpass those of Nahant in attractiveness.

With our boat safely moored one hundred yards from the northern cliffs we shall row ashore in the tender. It is high tide, and although it is a relatively calm day, the breakers are still dashing against the outer ledges. If we are careful, we can row in between the rocky cliffs to the entrance of the canal that extends across the eastern end of the island. We locate the opening after a few troubled minutes and finally pass between high cliffs with the noise of the breakers to the east diminishing at every stroke of the oars.

At last our craft gently slides up on the pebbly beach, which is covered with driftwood sufficient for many roaring bonfires. It is very quiet compared with the noise of the sea we have just left. We climb up the sides of the cliff and over to the southern side. Here the cliffs and chasms are of such grandeur and magnificence that they are more beautiful than anything else around Boston. Back in the western cove there is a peculiar rock which resembles a pulpit, and

Pulpit Rock has been pointed out for many years to visitors at the Brewsters. It is possible to explore many attractive little caves and inlets here at dead low tide.

But we must soon leave this beautiful spot, although a day could easily be spent here exploring the crags and cliffs. I like to think that an island similar to Outer Brewster, the prettiest in the outside Harbor, was in the mind of Thomas Haynes Bayley when he wrote:

> *Absence makes the heart grow fonder:*
> *Isle of beauty, fare thee well.*

INDEX

253

Index